A book that captures what real learning is all about. Thank you Ian, Ted, and Lee for sharing your knowledge and casting new insight on digital kids. A must read for every teacher, teaching in this modern, high-tech, digital, online world. This book equips teachers to meet these challenges and is the first of its kind to make a significant shift in focus from how teachers teach to how students learn.

Nicky Mohan, Developer, University of Waikato, New Zealand

In their new book, Jukes, McCain, and Crockett have broken new ground. While focusing on 21st-century skills—what they are now and will be in the future—this group has laid important groundwork for lifting our thinking into the 21st century. As they so aptly point out, we cannot correctly identify the skills for the 21st century with thinking still grounded in the 20th century. Jukes, McCain, and Crockett challenge our thinking first and then lead us to what is important for our students to be able to do in this new century. They are right on target for truly understanding the future of educating children.

Donna Walker Tileston, EdD, Author of *What Every Teacher Should Know*

Jukes, McCain, and Crockett have laid out an excellent road map for learning in the 21st century. After reading this, I am certain you will have a clearer understanding of this digital generation and why our classrooms continue to teach analog students in a digital world.

James Cisek, EdD

So you think your "digital" students live "unbalanced" lives? Ian, Ted, and Lee make the compelling argument that unless educators assimilate and understand the new digital technologies, they too may be "unbalanced" and poorly positioned to educate today's students.

Andrew Croll, Special Counsel and parent

Jukes, McCain, and Crockett ask thought-provoking questions to shift our thinking about 21st-century learning. This book offers concrete ideas for educators to find the balance between our past and our students' future, closing the gap between the digital native learning and the immigrant teaching environment. The correlation with learning and brain research is profound and provides insight for creating a rich digital teaching environment.

Pamela Lloyd, MEd, Director, GCI SchoolAccess

This book dramatically documents the need for educators to recognize that 21st-century learners do not learn like their predecessors. The included research and suggested strategies for change provide hope for the future. As a former Ohio school superintendent and staff development director, I believe it is a must read for those truly interested in educational reform.

Steve Franko, Strategic Planning and Professional Development Consultant

The students populating today's schools are fundamentally different from those of previous generations. If we are serious about educating them for life in the 21st century, we must acknowledge this difference and "rebalance" our approach to teaching them. In *Understanding the Digital Generation*, Ian, Ted, and Lee fully deliver on their goal of providing a greater understanding of the digital generation and sparking "deep thinking about how instruction should change to teach them effectively."

Brian Celli, MEd, Superintendent/CEO, Wild Rose School Division

Jukes, McCain, and Crockett offer up a highly readable, terribly important summary of the attributes of today's technologically enhanced children and explores the urgent implications for today's schools. Get this book and read it. And then pass it along to your administrators!

Doug Johnson, Director of Media and Technology, Mankato School District

While many assume 21st-century education merely demands access to hardware and the Internet, our greatest limit is one of pedagogical vision. Ian, Lee, and Ted consistently push us to re-imagine the entire premise of learning and collaboration in the future. Best of all, they know how to guide us through a strategic process that ensures our students will remain intellectually agile in a future that extends far beyond the traditional schoolhouse.

Christian Long, EdM, Educator, School Planner, Former President/CEO of DesignShare

Understanding the Digital Generation

Teaching and Learning in the New Digital Landscape

21st Century Fluency Project

Ian Jukes

Ian Jukes is the founder and director of the InfoSavvy Group, an international consulting firm. He has been a teacher at all grade levels; a school, district, and provincial administrator; a university instructor; and a national and international consultant. But first and foremost Ian is a passionate educational evangelist. To date he has written or co-written 12 books and 9 educational series and has had more than 200 articles published in various journals around the world. From the beginning, Ian's focus has been on the compelling need to restructure our educational institutions so that they become relevant to the current and future needs of children or, as David Thornburg writes, "to prepare them for their future and not just our past." That's why his materials tend to focus on the many pragmatic issues that provide the essential context for educational restructuring.

Ted McCain

Ted McCain is an educator who has taught high school students for 25 years. He has been an innovator and pioneer in technology education. He has designed courses for his school district and the province of British Columbia in computer science, data processing, desktop publishing, computer networking, web site design, digital animation, digital film effects, and sound engineering. In 1997, he received the Prime Minister's Award for Teaching Excellence. Ted has written or co-written seven books on the future, effective teaching, educational technology, and graphic design. His focus is on the impact on students and learning from the astounding changes taking place in the world today as a consequence of technological development.

Lee Crockett

Lee Crockett is a national award-winning designer, marketing consultant, entrepreneur, artist, author, and international keynote speaker. He is the director of media for the InfoSavvy Group and the managing partner of the 21st Century Fluency Project. He has co-authored three books with writers and educators Ian Jukes and Ted McCain. Lee is a "just in time learner" who is constantly adapting to the new programs, languages, and technologies associated with today's communications and marketing media. Understanding the need for balance in our increasingly digital lives, Lee has lived in Kyoto, Japan, where he studied Aikido and tea ceremony, as well as Florence, Italy, where he studied painting at the Accademia D'Arte.

I dedicate this book to the memory of my father, Arthur Hamilton Jukes, for all the love, support, and encouragement he gave me over the years; and to my son, Kyler, whom I have watched grow from child to man before my very eyes.

Ian Jukes

I dedicate this book to Sarah and Joel—my own digital kids who opened my eyes to things in the new digital world that I couldn't even imagine.

Ted McCain

I dedicate this book to the teachers, who ahead of their time stood apart, and aside, to let me learn my way—at warp speed.

Lee Crockett

There are many people who have supported us in the making of this book. Thank you Leigh, Deb, Belinda, Tomomi, Ross, Mae, Heather, Lori, Jason, Nikos, Janis, Matt, Nicky, James, Donna, Andrew, Pamela, Steve, Brian, Doug, Christian, and all the rest.

21st Century Fluency Project

co-published with

CORWIN
A SAGE Company

Cover Photo: ©iStockphoto.com/Pleio

For information:

21st Century Fluency Project Inc.
1685 Smithson Place
Kelowna BC Canada V1Y 8N5

www.21stcenturyfluency.com

ISBN 978-1-4495-8559-0 (pbk.)

Acquisitions Editor: Debra Stollenwerk
Editorial, Production, and Indexing: Abella Publishing Services, LLC
Typesetter: Ross Crockett
Cover Designer: Lee Crockett

 Table of Contents

21ˢᵗ Century Fluency Project

The 21st Century Fluency Project is about moving vision into practice through the process of investigating the effect of the last few decades on our society and particularly on our children, learning how we in education must adapt, and, finally, committing to meaningful changes at the classroom level.

Understanding the Digital Generation is the second book in our 21st Century Fluency Series. It is designed to help educators deal with the realities of teaching in the modern, high-tech, digital, online world.

A series of books, as well as related supporting materials, have been developed in order to answer five essential questions that teachers will ask when considering how educators and education must respond to the profound developments that are being experienced in the world at large. These questions are:

Why do I have to change?

Living on the Future Edge
The Impact of Global Exponential Trends on Education in the 21st Century

In this book, we discuss the power of paradigm to shape our thinking, the pressure that technological development is putting on our paradigm for teaching and learning, six global exponential trends in technological development that we can't ignore, what each of these trends means for education, new skills for students, new roles for teachers, and scenarios of education in the future.

Understanding the Digital Generation
Teaching and Learning in the New Digital Landscape

This book examines the effects that digital bombardment from constant exposure to electronic media has on children in the new digital landscape, and considers the profound implications this holds for the future of education. What does the latest neuroscientific and psychological research tell us about the role of intense and frequent experiences on the brain, particularly the young and impressionable brain?

Based on the research, what inferences can we make about children's digital experiences and how these experiences are rewiring and reshaping their cognitive processes? More important, what are the implications for teaching, learning, and assessment in the new digital landscape?

How can we reconcile these new developments with current instructional practices, particularly in a climate of standards and accountability driven by high-stakes testing for all? What strategies can we use to appeal to the learning preferences and communication needs of digital learners while at the same time honoring our traditional assumptions and practices related to teaching, learning, and assessment?

Where do I start?

The Digital Diet
Today's Digital Tools in Small Bytes

This book offers bite-sized, progressively challenging projects to introduce the reader to the digital landscape of today. This is the world of our children and students. *The Digital Diet* will help readers shed pounds of assumptions and boost their digital metabolism to help keep pace with these kids by learning to use some simple yet powerful digital tools.

How can I teach differently?

Teaching for Tomorrow
Teaching Content and Problem-Solving Skills

A key book in this series, *Teaching for Tomorrow* is a practical book for teachers struggling with how to teach 21st-century problem-solving skills while, at the same time, still covering the content in the curriculum guide. The book outlines a new teaching approach that significantly shifts the roles of the teacher and the student in learning. These new roles facilitate student ownership of learning. *Teaching for Tomorrow* also outlines the 4Ds problem-solving process, a process that students learn to use effectively as they become independent problem solvers.

What would this teaching look like in my classroom?

Literacy Is Not Enough
21st Century Fluencies for the Digital Age

It is no longer enough that we educate only to the standards of the traditional literacies of the 20th century. To be competent and capable in the 21st century requires a completely different set of skills above and beyond traditional literacies. These are the 21st-century fluencies that are identified and explained in detail in this book. The balance of the book introduces our framework for integrating these fluencies in our traditional curriculum and outlines a planning tool that can be used by educators to create their own 21st-century learning unit.

Curriculum Integration Kits

These kits are subject- and grade-specific publications designed to integrate the teaching of the 21st-century fluencies into today's curriculum and classroom. Included are detailed learning scenarios, resources, rubrics, and lesson plans with suggestions for high-tech, low-tech, or no-tech implementation. Also identified is the traditional content covered, as well as the standards and 21st-century fluencies each project covers.

The 21st Century Fluency Project Web Site
www.21stcenturyfluency.com

Our web site contains supplemental material that provides support for classroom teachers who are implementing 21st-century teaching. The site provides teachers with access to pre-made lesson plans that teach traditional content along with 21st-century fluencies. The site also offers teachers an online writing tool for designing their own lessons and teaching 21st-century fluencies, as well as other shared resources and a forum for additional collaboration and support.

How can we design effective schools for the 21st century?

Teaching the Digital Generation
No More Cookie Cutter High Schools

The world has changed. Young people have changed. But the same underlying assumptions about teachers, students, and instruction that have guided high school design for a hundred years continue to shape the way high schools are designed today. In fact, so much is assumed about the way a high school should look, that new schools continue to be created from a long-established template that is used without question. Strip away the skylights, the fancy foyers, and the high-tech P.A. systems, and most new schools being constructed today look pretty much the way they did when most adults went to school. This is a mismatch with reality. We need new designs that incorporate what we have learned about young people and how they learn best. This book outlines a new process for designing high schools and provides descriptions of several new models for how schools can be configured to better support learning.

Foreword

It's all about context.

To be effective at most things, we need to adapt our behavior to the context we are in, be it climate, dress, behavior, language, culture, or anything else. We might, occasionally and deliberately, do something that doesn't fit with the context, but doing so is most often counterproductive.

An important part of any teacher's job is to make sure students are aware of the context of their work, such as when we remind our students that spelling variations that are acceptable in a "texting" context are not acceptable in a more formal context (and vice versa), or that, in a math context, "find x" does not mean "circle it on the page."

Today, teachers ought to be thinking of context in a larger sense as well. Anyone living in a 21st-century world and teaching in a school classroom (a context we still, like it or not, have) knows those contexts are very different. Which is a better context in which to educate our young people—the classroom or the world? Or should they to be combined? Or is there yet another, better context for our young people's education? Finding the right answer to this question—that is, finding the best context for our students' education—is an issue that should concern us all. So what are our options?

At one end of the spectrum are those who think that the context of education remains the same "traditional" school that we have had for the past few hundred years (and that most of today's adults grew up with). For those people, it is the students' job to adapt to the context of the past (and present) school, to learn the standard curriculum in the traditional way (such as by listening and reading), and to do well on standardized tests. But even the people who promote this context know it is no longer educationally effective. The traditional methods of teaching are not producing the results we expect. Students see little in it that does, or will, apply to their real lives. The dropout rate is unacceptable. Sadly, the response of the believers in this context (which, even more sadly, includes too many of our politicians) is, "Do it better."

At the other end of the spectrum, and diverging quickly from the above, is another context—that in which our kids live their nonschool lives. I call this context "afterschool" (although some of it, like computer clubs, happens in our school buildings). For most kids in the developed world (and for many kids from other parts of the world as well—as Ian's lovely photo shows, p.15), this is a context filled with new technologies, new tools, new sources, and new possibilities. It is a context where kids teach themselves, follow their own interests, and prepare themselves on their own for the future.

Is the "after-school" context, in which kids live today, the context in which we should educate our kids? Many who believe this claim think that we no longer need schools at all. It is already a fact that everything any student needs to educate him- or herself in almost any area can be found on the Web in some form (such as much of YouTube plus the complete Yale and MIT curricula) and its presentation is getting better daily. All that is missing, say many of the after-school context proponents, is the motivation to use it. But even if the motivation were found, it would still leave the thorny questions of how to keep our kids safe while their parents work, how to support group activities, and how to integrate the perspectives of young people and adults.

What we really need to consider is yet another context for education, possibly the most important. That context is the world in which today's students will live their increasingly long lives after they leave school. Previously, that was never a separate context because the future in which our students would live was pretty much like the time they were educated.

But no longer. We know the future is changing exponentially and that, barring a world catastrophe, change is unlikely to slow down. It is likely that the technology of our students' future lives will be as much as a trillion times more powerful than today's. From the perspective of today's educators and planners, the future our students will be living in will be, in many respects, almost totally science fictional. Yet it will still involve (I hope and expect) people interacting and learning from each other. Fortunately, new "partnering" pedagogies have emerged that work much better within this context of rapid change.

If you are a teacher, administrator, or other educator caught between the demands of today's in-school context (No Child Left Behind), today's "after-school" context (kids learning on their own, using lots of technology), and the context of our students' lives tomorrow, how do you find your way?

My suggestion is to put yourself in the position of a student in today's and future educational contexts and their implications. As such, you need to widely scan the environment and make your own judgments about what is already here and what is coming. This book will help you do that.

The authors of this book believe—as I do—that, while it is key that we retain some essentials of the past, our true job as educators is to prepare our students for the rest of their lives. Some of what the authors report and claim in this book is still controversial, and some of the information they cite we may not totally agree with. But whether one accepts every detail or not, the authors are pointing us, I strongly believe, in the right direction.

If you agree with Ian, Ted, Lee, and me that the context for education is radically and rapidly changing, then, to be an effective teacher (that is, a helper, guide, coach, and preparer of individuals who will live in that context), you will want to adapt to that new context yourself. Not because anyone says "you should" or "you must." But rather because your own self-respect as a professional, and your concern for the needs of the students you teach, compel you to do no less.

Marc Prensky

 Introduction

In the first book of this series, *Living on the Future Edge*, we made the case for the overwhelming need to change the traditional mode of instruction used in schools today because our world has changed significantly since our school system was originally designed.

In *Understanding the Digital Generation*, we make the case for changing current instructional practices. We argue that the existing school system was not designed for the digital generation that has been profoundly affected by the digital online world. If we want to redesign instruction to keep it relevant and effective in the 21st century, then we must take a long look at this generation and acknowledge that they are not the students that traditional schools were originally designed for.

Children today are different! Not just because they mature years earlier than children did even a couple of generations ago. Not just because of the clothes they wear or don't wear. Not just because they dye their hair and style it differently than we did when we were that age. And not just because they seem to have more body parts than we did—which they seem to want to pierce, tattoo, and/or expose.

No, today's digital generation is different because it has grown up in a new digital landscape. For most of the digital generation, there has never been a time in their lives when they haven't been surrounded by computers, digital video, cell phones, video games, the Internet, online tools, and all the other digital wonders that increasingly define their (and our) world. Constant exposure to digital media has changed the way the digital generation processes, interacts, and uses information. As a result, they think and communicate in fundamentally different ways than any previous generation.

Meanwhile, many adults are struggling to keep up as they try to come to terms with the rapid change, powerful new technologies, and changes in thinking in the world that kids take for granted. This is a fundamentally different world than the one we grew up in.

This book examines the new digital landscape and the profound implications that it holds for the future of education. In Part I, we discuss the gap between the life experience of kids today and that of their parents and teachers. We also summarize what the latest neuroscience and psychological research tell us about how the digital generation's brains are being rewired.

In Part II, we discuss the implications the arrival of new digital students will have for teaching, learning, and assessment.

From the outset, it is important for you to understand that this is not a "how-to" book with lots of ready-to-use examples that can be immediately implemented in a classroom. This is a book of concepts that will lay the foundation for the practical material that follows in subsequent books in this series. Our hope is that this material will truly help you to understand the digital generation and spark deep thinking about how instruction should change to teach them effectively.

Part I

Understanding the Digital Generation

Chapter 1

The Need for Balance

> The trouble with our times is that the future is not what it used to be.
>
> **Paul Valery**

"What's wrong with kids today?"

"Kids today aren't as smart as they were when I was young."

"Students today can't read the way students did 20 years ago."

"Kids are addicted to the Internet, and because of that, they are losing their social skills."

"All these kids want to do is play their video games."

"When I ask students for the capital city of Peru, they say they don't know, they'll just Google it. They just don't seem to be able to learn the way students used to. And what's Googling got to do with learning anyway?"

"These kids just can't concentrate the way that kids used to. They just won't sit and listen."

"All students want to do today is look at videos on YouTube, photos on Flickr, chat on Facebook, and play games. They have lost the ability to focus on the real skills that will help them in the future."

These are just a few of the actual responses we have heard when talking to teachers about the students in their classes today. There is great concern over the students' lack of ability to learn the way students have in the past, especially from teachers who have been teaching for some time. Many teachers have told us their teaching is just not as effective with the students in their classrooms today as it once was, which is creating a groundswell of concern. Something is different. In this book, we want to explore exactly what is different about kids today and what is causing the changes we see in their behavior.

A Serious Concern Over the Lack of Balance in the Lives of Kids Today

One of the most common responses we get from adults when we give presentations on the topic of the digital generation is that there appears to be a lack of balance in the lives of young people, who spend most of their time outside school texting people on their cell phones, chatting with friends using instant messaging, interacting with people on Facebook or MySpace, playing games on Xbox or Wii, and surfing the Internet.

We agree there are significant concerns, and it is necessary that we point out not everything digital is better. For this book to be of real value to teachers and parents, it is important that the positive benefits of using online digital tools be counterbalanced with the negative effects that accompany their use. There are some serious and legitimate concerns over what the digital world is doing to the minds of the young people who are immersed in it.

One book that does an excellent job of outlining the issues surrounding digital culture is *iBrain: Surviving the Technological Alteration of the Modern Mind* by Gary Small and Gigi Vorgon (2008). Small is a neuroscientist and his points are based on brain studies that he and other neuroscientists conducted. Another book based on brain research that documents some of the negative aspects of technology use is *Brain Rules* by John Medina (2008). We will quote extensively from these books to underscore some of the major concerns that have arisen over the excessive use of digital tools.

A major theme of our book is that the digital world is changing the way kids think—their brains are being altered by the audiovisual and interactive experiences provided by new online digital tools. This has been confirmed by research. Small begins his book with the following statement:

> *Daily exposure to high technology—computers, smart phones, video games, search engines like Google and Yahoo—stimulates brain cell alteration and neurotransmitter release, gradually strengthening new neural pathways in our brains while weakening old ones. Because of the current technological revolution, our brains are evolving right now—at a speed like never before.*
> (Small & Vorgon, 2008, p. 1)

This rapid alteration of the brain has already been so drastic that traditional thinking about cognitive development is proving inadequate to describe what is occurring in the brains of children today. Jean Piaget made observations on a child's cognitive development well over one hundred years ago that have been very useful in understanding what is going on inside a child's brain as he or she ages. However, the rapid evolution of the brain that is occurring today is making many reconsider the validity of traditional thought on cognitive development. Small makes the following statement regarding this dramatic change in the brains of children today:

> *The nineteenth-century French psychologist Jean Piaget charted these milestones to adulthood, beginning with the first two years of life, when a toddler develops awareness of other people and learns to relate to them. From two to six years, the young child learns basic language skills. However, the thinking is relatively concrete until the teen years, when the ability for abstract thought and reason takes hold. If digital technology continues to distract young susceptible minds at the present rate, the traditional developmental stages will need to be redefined.*
> (Small & Vorgon, 2008, p. 28)

This redefinition will more accurately describe what is happening in the brains of young people as their minds respond to the new experiences provided by digital tools. It will also highlight a growing concern over whether important cognitive milestones are being delayed or missed entirely as kids grow up in a digital culture. While the advanced skills they develop in the use of digital tools empower them to do remarkable things and, in many ways, will serve them well in the future, there are concerns that important cognitive skills are not being developed while they devote their attention to the digital world, to the exclusion of other things.

One important skill area that is underdeveloped in a digital culture is face-to-face interpersonal interaction. Kids today are spending more time interacting with online virtual relationships or digital tools and less time interacting with real people in face-to-face relationships. A major concern is what this decreased face-to-face interpersonal interaction is doing to brain development and the acquisition of interpersonal skills. Following are two quotes from Small that highlight this concern.

> *Without enough face-to-face interpersonal stimulation, a child's neural circuits can atrophy, and the brain may not develop normal interactive social skills.* (Small & Vorgon, 2008, p. 27)

> *Recent neuroscience points to pathways in the brain that are necessary to hone interpersonal skills, empathetic abilities, and effective personal instincts. In the digital generation, which has been raised on technology, these interpersonal neural pathways are often left unstimulated and underdeveloped.* (Small & Vorgon, 2008, p. 117)

While it is clear that skills in creating and maintaining virtual relationships are important in the modern world, it is also clear that those skills must be balanced with doing the same thing in face-to-face relationships if young people are going to have satisfying and productive interactions with others, both personally and professionally.

Another concern has arisen over one of the most noticeable traits of the digital generation—multitasking. They are always performing multiple digital tasks simultaneously—surfing the Internet, watching a video, chatting online with friends using instant messaging, and downloading music at the same time, all while they are also doing their homework.

Kids develop the ability to perform these multiple tasks as they grow up in the online digital world. What they can do is impressive and can be very useful in a digital culture. However, it's not always a good thing to multitask. The problem arises when someone has to do a task that is new to them and requires concentration to accomplish, such as many of the tasks students must do in school. Trying to multitask while attempting to complete a challenging new task goes against our biology.

> *Research shows that we can't multitask. We are biologically incapable of processing attention-rich inputs simultaneously. We must jump from one thing to the next.* (Medina, 2008, p. 85)

Essentially, trying to do many things at once means we have to interrupt the brain from doing one thing to switch to do something else. This constant switching can be problematic when trying to complete a specific task because valuable time is lost as we move from one endeavor to another.

> *Neuroscientists have found that we lose time during these switches, especially when a task is new or unfamiliar.* (Small & Vorgon, 2008, p. 68)

Researchers looking into a person's productivity have discovered that the attention loss that results from switching between tasks causes people to take longer to complete tasks and that they make more errors than those who do not multitask.

> *Studies show that a person who is interrupted takes 50 percent longer to accomplish a task. Not only that, he or she makes up to 50 percent more errors.* (Medina, 2008, p. 87)

Medina goes on to say that the effect of multitasking on productivity is like trying to get something done after you've had several stiff drinks. We might think we are doing really well, when in reality we are slower and sloppier and we make many more mistakes. It is important that we teach our students how to apply themselves to increase productivity and reduce errors. Small and Vorgon (2008) point out that while multitasking is an essential skill in the digital world, to minimize the negative aspects of doing multiple tasks simultaneously, we must balance multitasking with strategies for developing single-tasking skills as well.

> *Multitasking has become a necessary skill of modern life, but we need to acknowledge the challenges and adapt accordingly. Several strategies can help, such as striving to stay on one task longer, and avoiding task switching whenever possible.* (Small & Vorgon, 2008, p. 69)

There are concerns over the ability of the digital generation to stay with and follow a long and complex argument. The rapid access, skim, and leave reading behavior fostered by surfing the Internet, coupled with the multitasking that is done in the digital world, has made the digital generation less likely to work their way through documents that require a more patient approach to follow the thought of longer and more challenging opinions and arguments.

Small talks about partial continuous attention, a different state of mind related to multitasking. Partial continuous attention results from the bombardment of information that assaults the senses in the digital world. There is so much going on from text messages to Internet videos to music to cell phone calls to brightly colored flashing web sites to instant messages that a person's mind is continually skimming and skipping to keep track of it all. This butterfly brain activity can be a real problem when trying to get students to focus on important work in school and for getting employees to focus on their work.

The increasing time that kids spend using their digital tools is having negative effects on several other areas of their development. There is great concern that young people are not getting enough physical exercise. Coupled with the lack of physical activity, there is legitimate concern that they are not gaining an appreciation for nature and being in the outdoors. Many parents and teachers worry that young people are not spending enough time reading for pleasure or reading at all for that matter. There are concerns that the highly addictive nature of computer games, online adventure sites, and the interactive nature of most digital activities are creating such obsessive behavior in kids that it meets the definition of a clinical addiction.

These are just a few of the concerns that have been raised over the effects of the digital world on the minds and behavior of people immersed in digital culture. As we will state many times in this book, new digital tools provide powerful new ways for getting things done, and developing skills in using them is essential in the modern world. But while acquiring these skills is important, it is clear that young people must have balance in their lives in order to develop into fully functional and productive friends, spouses or partners, colleagues, and citizens.

The Need for Balance in the Lives of Adults

Balance cuts two ways, however. Adult parents, teachers, administrators, school district staff, community members, and politicians are all involved in making decisions about what students will learn, how they will learn, where they will learn, what facilities they will use, what programs will be funded, what equipment they will use, and how their performance will be evaluated. And yet many of these same people have not spent much, if any, time learning about the realities of the new online digital world that has radically altered the leisure activities of young people, the world of work, and the minds of the students they are mandated to prepare for life in the future. These adults live very unbalanced lives themselves, and unless they counterbalance their old nondigital life experiences with new digital experiences, it will have catastrophic consequences for education.

How can we expect students to remain interested in schools based on 20th-century ideas of what learning looks like? How can we expect students to see the relevance of instructional approaches that target outdated skills? How can we think we are connecting with the digital generation when the examples we use in our learning materials and our instruction come from a nondigital time that these kids can't relate to? How can we think we are adequately preparing students for life in the 21st century if we have not learned how the 21st-century world operates? And how can we expect our students to follow our advice about how to conduct themselves when we have not entered their world in any meaningful way?

We agree with all those adults who are crying out for balance in the lives of young people today. It is urgently needed. But we are also crying out for balance in the lives of the adults who are in control of the school system—balance that embraces the realities of the digital online world, balance that acknowledges the kids are way ahead of us, and balance that recognizes we have a lot of learning to do before we can effectively apply our life experience to guide our students in this new digital world. In fact, that is exactly what our goal is in writing this book—to create balance in the lives of adults so our schools can be effective in teaching the young minds of today and tomorrow the wonderful things we have to share that will make them well-rounded, thoughtful, productive, and creative people.

Summarizing the Main Points

- There is a serious lack of balance in the lives of kids today.

- The rapid evolution of the brain that is occurring due to digital technology is causing many to reconsider the validity of traditional thought on cognitive development.

- One important skill area that is underdeveloped in a digital culture is face-to-face interpersonal interaction.

- Children today need to balance multitasking with strategies for developing single-tasking skills as well.

- Adults must counterbalance their old nondigital life experiences with new digital experiences or there will be catastrophic consequences for education.

 ## Some Questions to Consider

- How has your world changed in the past 30 years? How is your life different now than it was then?

- What technology do you use today that you didn't have 20 years ago, or even 10 years ago?

- How many of those new technologies can you now carry with you?

- What devices and services that once required a human operator have now been automated?

- How has the appearance of this new digital landscape affected you, your family, your community, and your workplace?

Reading and References

Dryden, G., & Vos, J. (2009). *Unlimited: The new learning revolution and the seven keys to unlock it.* Auckland, New Zealand: The Learning Web.

Johnson, S. (2005). *Everything bad is good for you: How today's popular culture is actually making us smarter.* New York: Riverhead.

Medina, J. (2008). *Brain rules: 12 principles for surviving and thriving at work, home, and school.* Seattle, WA: Pear Press.

Pink, D. (2005). *A whole new mind: Moving from the information age to the conceptual age.* New York: Riverhead.

Small, G., & Vorgon, G. (2008). *iBrain: Surviving the technological alteration of the modern mind.* New York: Harper Collins.

Tapscott, D. (2009). *Grown up digital: How the net generation is changing your world.* New York: McGraw-Hill.

Chapter 2
The Problem of the Gap

> Nostalgia is like a grammar lesson: You find the present tense and the past perfect.
>
> **Robert Orben**

There is a huge problem in our schools today. This problem is not readily apparent when you take a quick look as students arrive at school, go to their lockers, saunter into their classrooms, and sit as their teachers begin their lessons, but it's there.

The problem is the rapidly growing gap of understanding between the young people sitting in the classrooms and the adults who teach them and make decisions about what they will learn, where they will learn, and how they will learn. The problem is that this gap in understanding is causing a crisis of relevance in our schools. If it is not addressed, then we fear for the long-term viability of the public school system because many alternatives to traditional schooling are now appearing in the new digital world.

We believe it is critical to examine the nature of this gap. To do this, it is important to explore some aspects of the life today's adults experienced when they were young and compare it to the life young people experience today. It is essential to do this in order to grasp the magnitude of the gap that has developed between these new digital kids and previous generations. By describing the nature of this gap, we can establish a foundation for making significant changes to the way we teach the digital generation.

Connecting With Students Is a Key to Effective Teaching

Understanding what kids are going through is a key to effective parenting and teaching. This knowledge helps us have empathy and compassion for our children and students. For teachers, being able to draw upon an understanding of the world students are experiencing helps us use examples and illustrations that connect with what students know and with the joys and difficulties they encounter every day. Brain research tells us this connection is a key to effective instruction.

For much of the 20th century, the world experienced by children was not radically different from the world that was experienced by their parents and teachers. Yes, there were new inventions like radio or television, but the fundamental approach to life did not change. Teachers could assume that much of their experience growing up was still valid for their students. Teachers could use examples from their own youth with confidence that their students would understand them. It was common for adults to think they understood kids because they were once in the same position, going though the same things the kids were going though.

However, something of great significance has happened in the world since most of us were children. It was the rapid emergence of the online digital world. This new, networked world of instantaneous access to information and communication around the globe exploded onto the scene in the mid-1990s. The experiences available to kids growing up today are so different from what the vast majority of adults experienced in their youth that a significant gap in understanding has developed in the short time this online digital world has been in existence. This new digital world has rendered much of what adults experienced as children disconnected and inapplicable to the world of modern kids.

This gap in understanding is already a huge problem for educators. Traditional instruction is not working as effectively as it once did in our schools. Worse, students are turning off and tuning out because the adults in control of the system are making decisions based on an outdated idea of what growing up is like. And this crisis is only getting worse with each passing day because the online digital world of kids is changing, growing, adapting, and innovating with astonishing speed. It is absolutely critical that anyone involved in teaching students or making decisions that affect the teaching of students takes the time to bridge this gap in understanding between themselves and the world of kids today.

The first step in understanding how we need to change to educate the digital generation is to take a look at ourselves. We need to identify the snapshot we have in our heads of what we think growing up looks like because it colors so much of our thinking about students and how to teach them.

The Problem of Our Past

In our book, *Living on the Future Edge* (Jukes, McCain, & Crockett, 2010), we discussed the concept of exponentialism at length. The exponential development of technological power has reached the point where the magnitude and speed of change is altering modern life so radically it makes it difficult to keep up. Life changes so fast that everyone alive today finds themselves holding on to outdated ideas for how things are done. No matter how old you are, you can remember the "good old days." Let's take a quick walk down memory lane to see what you remember from your youth.

Some of you may be old enough to remember toys with brightly colored lead paints, or maybe you can remember riding bikes without helmets, or riding in the back of a pickup truck on a warm summer night. Maybe you can remember playing outside in the sun all day, without sunscreen, and drinking from a garden hose when you got thirsty, or sharing a soda from a bottle with friends and not getting sick. Maybe you can remember walking to school and the corner store, running through a sprinkler, and sprinting after the ice cream truck.

Perhaps you can remember sitting down for a family meal almost every night and discussing things with your parents and siblings. You might even remember when your mom (and most of the other moms) stayed home while your dad went to work. Maybe you can remember when one of the very worst things that could ever happen to you was being sent to your room because there was absolutely nothing to do in there other than reflect on your crimes.

Depending on your age, you may remember having only one television in your house, or only three channels to watch. You might even remember getting your first color television or your first television with a remote control. Maybe you can remember sitting with your family to watch television programs together. Perhaps you remember Saturday morning cartoons like Bugs Bunny, Transformers, or Rocky and Bullwinkle. You might remember a time when the only ways to watch a movie were to go to the movie theater or the video store to rent one.

Maybe you can remember slick technology like 33- and 45-rpm records, or when they were replaced with cassettes and eight tracks, or when those were replaced with CDs. Perhaps you can remember using 5¼-inch or 3½-inch floppy disks in computers. Maybe you had a dot matrix printer at work or in your home. You might remember cell phones that could only make phone calls. Or you might remember computers that were not connected to the Internet. Perhaps you can remember when the World Wide Web was new and limited in scope. Maybe you can remember something as archaic as sending a handwritten letter.

> *. . . most of the people reading this book grew up in a radically different time than the one kids experience today.*

You might remember when your teachers were authorities to be respected—when they disciplined students with a ruler and the strap. Perhaps you can remember when teachers and textbooks were the only sources of information in the classroom. You might be able to think back to when doing research was a largely physical act that involved going to the library, using the Dewey Decimal System to search the card catalog, and then wandering through the stacks of books, hoping to find what you were looking for. If you were lucky enough to locate the book you wanted, you then flipped through it trying to find the needed information. Some of you might remember handwriting your lab reports and essays.

Your memories may be slightly different, but we hope you get the idea. Regardless of how old you are, most of the people reading this book grew up in a radically different time than the one kids experience today. For the vast majority of adult educators, at least part of what we have just outlined was your experience of life and learning when you grew up.

It is very important that you understand the impact these experiences have on your ideas for how families operate, how businesses run, how society works, what kids do with their recreation time, what teaching looks like, what skills and knowledge should be valued in school, where you get new information when you need it, what that information looks like, how you relate to other people, who has authority in life, and what you need to do to be successful. It is critical that you understand that these experiences have formed a powerful mindset that you carry with you throughout life, including how you think in the classroom, in the staff room, at staff meetings, at school district planning meetings, at school board meetings, and on political committees.

Why is knowing this so important? If we are going to understand the huge gap that has developed between us and the digital generation who have emerged since the mid-1990s, then we need to identify both sides of this gap of understanding. Therefore, it is important to honestly assess the snapshot we have in our memories of what it is like to be young, to entertain ourselves, to go to school, to interact with others, and to experience the adult world. Further, if we are going to adapt and adjust our teaching to be relevant to these kids, we must identify the reasons we do the things we do in schools today. And the reasons we do so many of those things are rooted deeply in the past of the adults who are in control of the school system—a past that is radically different from the current reality experienced by kids growing up today.

That Was Then, This Is Now

The world young people experience today is a very different place than the one we grew up in. It's a world constantly on the move. It's no longer the stable place that many of us experienced. Consider the changing nature of families. During the past 30 years, the number of families being led by a single parent has increased dramatically. Beyond that, we now have blended families, interracial families, gay and lesbian families, families separated or multiplied by divorce, or just about any other possible combination you can imagine. The everyday world is different.

Our rhythm of life is now dictated as much by work schedules as by family needs. There was a time not that long ago when it was unusual to have both parents working, when the workweek was five days, and nothing was open on Sunday. According to the Boston College Center for Work and Family report, "Defining Paternity Leave: Shifting Roles, New Responsibilities in the Family and the Workplace in 1977" (Sylvia DeMott & Kathy Lynch, 2004),49 percent of fathers had wives who also worked outside of the home. In 2002, 67 percent of fathers were part of a dual-earner marriage.

Today we live in a 24/7/365 world, where routines are harder to maintain. Family meals, family time, one-on-one time, quiet time, down time, and days off are more difficult to schedule than ever. As a result, life today has developed a fast-food mentality, both literally and figuratively.

A 2006 Media family report written by Victoria Rideout and Elizabeth Hamel titled "The Media Family: Electronic Media in the Lives of Infants, Toddlers, Preschoolers, School Age Children and Their Parents," a week in the life of an average school-age child includes .5 hour with dad, 2.6 hours with mom, 2.2 hours doing homework, .5 hour reading for pleasure, and more than 25 hours—near the equivalent of a full-time job or a week of school—watching television, playing video games, and interacting with digital devices.

As a result of this changing world, parents today spend 40 percent less time with their children than parents did just 30 years ago, and much of that time is spent watching television and movies. The scarcest resource for many families today is not time, but attention. Consequently, there's a growing void in children's lives that is being filled by technology. This isn't an overnight trend. There has been a steady progression as parents have had less time to spend with their children. It started years ago with the telephone, radio, and television. It then progressed to videos and video games. Now it's online gaming, email, surfing, online chatting, cell phones, blogging, texting, and a growing host of other digital experiences.

Today, a growing percentage of children come home from school to no one, because either both parents or their only parent is at work (Martin, et al., 2004). Consequently, many children are left to their own "devices," and for a number of reasons, including safety concerns, instead of playing on the street or at the park, many children now stay inside watching television or videos, listening to music, playing video games, texting, blogging, talking on the phone, and surfing the Internet. In our 24/7/365 world, these new digital gizmos have become the babysitters, the constant companions, and best friends, for many children.

These devices are increasingly where today's digital generation find their role models and learn their social skills. Their rooms are filled with people, relationships, interactions, and adventures that come through their computers, phones, and video games. This generation is more comfortable with virtual, screen-to-screen relationships than they are with face-to-face relationships.

Children today view world events as they occur. They see history in the making.

While the worst thing that could have happened to many people of our generation was to be sent to their rooms, many children today are completely comfortable nesting in their digital cocoons, otherwise known as their bedrooms. Today's world is decidedly more high-tech than our world was when we were growing up. According to a Pew Internet and Life Project study titled "Teens and Social Media" (Lenhart, Madden, Smith, & Macgill, 2007), some 93 percent of teens use the Internet, 82 percent of American children play video games on a regular basis—an average of 8.2 hours per week—and more than 70 percent of dollars spent by children and teenagers on toys are spent on electronic games.

Today's children take for granted having access to computers, remote controls, the Internet, email, cell phones, mp3 players, online movies, video games, and digital cameras. These are tools and toys with capabilities that would have been unimaginable when we were children, let alone even 10 years ago. As a result, for the digital generation, there's never been a time where these digital wonders haven't existed. They haven't just adopted digital media, they've internalized it.

Kids growing up today live in a 600-channel television universe. It's a 10,000-station radio universe accessible online. It's a universe with a 1,000,000,000,000 (one trillion) plus page Internet (Google, 2008). Children today view world events as they occur. They see history in the making. They watch events like the collapse of the World Trade Center, the invasion of Iraq, the Sumatran tsunami, the eruption of an Indonesian volcano, or a hurricane in the American south in real time as they were happening halfway around the world. Consequently, the notion of time and distance, which meant so much to us, means very little to kids today. This generation operates at what Marc Prensky (2006) describes as "twitch speed." Children accept instantaneous access to information, goods, and services at the click of a mouse as normal. They expect to be able to communicate with anyone or anything at any time and anywhere.

Such everyday expectations have led to the death of patience and the emergence of a society increasingly expecting and demanding instant gratification. This is one of the reasons why it is more difficult to get children to read printed text today. Reading is a delayed gratification medium, while television, video games, and the Internet are immediate gratification media.

Such assumptions and expectations about instantaneous access are the result of a massive shift of information and services to the Internet. Today, from a desktop, laptop, or cell phone, children have instantaneous access to virtually every library, art gallery, and museum in the world. More important to them, these children also have access to friends, games, music, movies, shopping, cheat sheets, and tens of thousands of online sites specifically designed to attract the digital generation.

Because they've grown up with not just text-based information, but also images, sounds, color, and video presented as a single entity, this generation has developed an MTV mindset. For them, as David Thornburg (2000) suggests, this isn't multimedia, it's monomedia. It has all been reduced to digital zeroes and ones. If you think that Sesame Street had an effect on how kids thought in the past, you can imagine what a different effect exposure to interactive television, computers, cell phones, the Internet, and video games is having on the digital generation.

Children today are completely comfortable with the visual bombardment of simultaneous images, text, and sounds because, for them, such experiences provide relevant and compelling experiences that can convey more information in a few seconds than can be communicated by reading an entire book. Moreover, these new media are not just designed for passive viewing, because passive viewing just doesn't cut it. This generation no longer wants just to be the audience; they want to be the actors. They expect, want, and need interactive information, interactive resources, interactive communications, and relevant, real-life experiences.

This trend does not just apply to those who have access to the latest digital media or the Internet. It also applies to the technological have-nots, the disadvantaged children on the other side of the so-called digital divide, who still have access to video games, cell phones, mp3 players, and a multitude of other digital gadgets. In fact, this trend isn't unique to North American children, but is pervasive around the world regardless of socioeconomics, culture, race, or religion.

For example, Ian recently took a picture in the 300-year-old Arab market in Singapore. It is hard to describe the sensory experience to someone who has never experienced the Arab market. The sights, sounds, and smells of the street are absolutely overwhelming. According to the locals, other than electricity and automobiles, the scene is little different than it was three centuries ago. The picture he took was of an 11-year-old girl who was sitting on a bolt of cloth patiently waiting while her mother bartered for fabric. In her hand was a palm-sized wireless device she was using to surf the Internet.

For this digital generation, it's second nature to multitask. They can do their homework, talk on the phone, listen to music, download movies, surf the Internet, and maintain multiple, simultaneous conversations about last night's American Idol on a chat line—and still be bored.

Increasingly, today's children are immersed in electronic and visual media. They use digital technology transparently, without thinking about it, marveling at it, or wondering about how it works. This is the first generation that has ever mastered the tools essential to society before the older generations. They are the digital generation.

Because they have grown up in this new digital landscape with constant exposure to digital devices, and because of this chronic digital bombardment, digital is their first language—their native tongue. As we discuss in *Living on the Future Edge* (Jukes, McCain, & Crockett, 2010), we are at a moment in history where the global exponential trends driving the technological revolution are turning vertical. These changes have been so recent and so extreme that, whether you grew up in the 1960s or in the 1990s, you most likely did not grow up with this digital bombardment.

As Prensky (2006) points out, most people from our generation and our parents' generation are not from the digital generation. We don't speak digital as a first language.

Young girl in market, Singapore, September 2007; photograph by Ian Jukes.

The people of our generation come from the old country. We come from the nondigital world. We come from a time and place before digital technology changed just about everything. Because of our relatively stable, text-based, lower-tech upbringing, we have old-country traditions and assumptions about the world. We don't speak digital as a first language (DFL), but rather digital as a second language (DSL). We speak digital as a second language and with varying degrees of skill.

Like all immigrants, some of us are better than others at adapting to the ways of the new country, but like all immigrants, we retain some degree of our accent from the old country. Some of us have caught on quickly and thrive in this new country, while others struggle to apply old thinking to new ways of doing things, new technologies, and new mindsets. Communicating in this new language can be a challenge for us, and the thicker our accent, the harder it is to be understood by the digital generation.

You know you're DSL if you talk about dialing a number or buying a new album, if you need a manual to learn new software or a phone book to find a number, if you print out email to read it or a report to edit it, or if you go to the library to find technical information.

You couldn't live or work in another country unless you resided there and learned the language, customs, and culture. In much the same way, if we don't learn to speak the digital language, customs, and culture of our students, we will experience a digital disconnect with many of them. In fact, many educators already have. Consciously or unconsciously, many of the digital generation sense that most of their teachers aren't a part of, are not in sync with, and probably don't understand the world in which they live.

As people of our generation, many of us are distracted and disoriented by multiple, simultaneous information sources and random access. We need to read a manual, take a course, or talk face-to-face. Although we may use the digital tools, they're not always intuitive and their use does not always come naturally. The digital generation, on the other hand, picks up new devices and starts experimenting with them right away. They assume the inherent design of the devices will teach them how to use a new gadget intuitively. This is because the digital generation has adopted a mindset of rapid-fire trial-and-error learning. They're not afraid of making mistakes because they learn more quickly that way. They operate under the strategy of useful failure and have no problem sourcing help online, while people of our generation often operate under the assumption that all failure is bad and help comes from an expert or a book.

Many people of our generation just can't understand how anyone can learn by experimentation. By the time they have read the table of contents of a manual, the digital generation has already figured out 15 things that will work and 15 things that don't. People of our generation are afraid of breaking the device; the digital generation knows there is a reset button. People of our generation focus on and try to apply the skills learned in another time.

As Steven Johnson (2005) repeatedly points out in his marvelous book, *Everything Bad Is Good for You: How Today's Popular Culture Is Actually Making Us Smarter*, we often don't appreciate the skill development of the digital generation—skills they have honed to perfection with years of trial-and-error practice.

What some of us don't understand is that the reason the digital generation has different skills and literacies is that there has been a profound shift in the kind of skills used and needed to operate in the digital world. The reason their skill development is different is because their focus is different. They are developing skills in areas other than we did and we often don't acknowledge or see the value these skills have. Instead, we complain about the skills they don't have. Because digital isn't our native language and because we're immigrants to their world, many of us believe children who act differently need to be fixed.

The digital generation has a completely new and different set of skills than the ones we have and value. They don't need to be fixed; rather, we need to use and build on the new skills they bring to the classroom. People of our generation were taught to value tradition, and we may unconsciously believe that the skills of the digital generation are not as good as ours or that they're not as literate as we are because they don't appear to value or prioritize our literacies. We must take a moment to realize we are not in our world anymore. This is a new digital world. It's not going back to the way it was. We, as parents and educators, must accept this, because this new world infused with technology is having a significant impact on the way kids today think (which we will discuss in more detail in Chapter 3). More than ever, the digital generation needs our guidance and wisdom to help them shape the future for all of us.

Summarizing the Main Points

- Our lives growing up were lower tech than today.
- We entertained ourselves with our imaginations.
- Our games were "active" and mostly played outside.
- Our lives were stable and predictable.
- Our parents were very present in our lives.
- We did many things together as a family.
- We had little complex access to knowledge.
- Teachers and school were the experts and the authority.

Some Questions to Consider

- Describe some of your favorite memories of growing up and how those experiences differ with the reality of growing up today.
- What foods and drinks did you enjoy that you don't, won't, or can't eat today?
- What toys and equipment did you play with? How do those things compare with the toys and equipment kids have today?
- Reflect on your childhood. Identify some of the favorite musical groups at that time. Who were the major political figures? What were the major drivers of the economy? What were the standard technologies being used in offices? What were the major means of communication?
- Describe the schools of your youth. What did they look like? How were they organized? What was the focus? What were the major forms of instruction? What were the major technologies?
- How do the schools of your childhood contrast with the schools of today?

Reading and References

Bauerlein, M. (2008). *The dumbest generation: How the digital age stupefies young Americans and jeopardizes our future (Or, don't trust anyone under 30)*. New York: Tarcher.

DeMott, S., & Lynch, K., (2004) *Defining paternity leave: Shifting roles, new responsibilities in the family and the workplace* Menlo Park, CA: Kaiser Family Foundation.

Dryden, G., & Vos, J. (2009). *Unlimited: The new learning revolution and the seven keys to unlock it*. Auckland, New Zealand: The Learning Web.

Goodstein, A. (2007). *Totally wired: What teens and tweens are really doing online*. New York: St. Martin's Griffin.

http://googleblog.blogspot.com/2008/07/we-knew-web-was-big.html

Johnson, S. (2005). *Everything bad is good for you: How today's popular culture is actually making us smarter*. New York: Riverhead.

Jukes, I. , McCain, T., & Crockett L. (2010). *Living on the future edge: The impact of global exponential trends on education in the 21st century*. Kelowna, BC: 21st Century Fluency Project.

Kandel, E. (2006). *In search of memory: The emergence of a new science of mind*. London: W.W. Norton.

McCain, T., & Jukes, I. (2000). *Windows on the future: Education in the age of technology*. Thousand Oaks, CA: Corwin.

Rideout, V. & Hamel, E., (2006) *The media family: Electronic media in the lives of infants, toddlers, preschoolers, school age children and their parents*. Chestnut Hill, MA: Boston College.

Lenhart, A., Madden, M., Smith, A., & Macgill, A., (2007) *Teens and Social Media*. Washington, DC: Pew Research Center's Internet & American Life Project.

Pink, D. (2005). *A whole new mind: Moving from the information age to the conceptual age*. New York: Riverhead.

Prensky, M. (2006). *Don't bother me mom—I'm learning*. St. Paul, MN: Paragon House.

Thornburg, D. (2000). As quoted in October 14 2000, CUE California Conference Speech, San Carlos CA.

Tapscott, D. (2009). *Grown up digital: How the net generation is changing your world*. New York: McGraw-Hill.

U.S. Census Bureau, (2007) *Current population survey, 2006: Annual social and economic supplement*. http://www.census.gov/apsd/techdoc/cps/cpsmar06.pdf

Willingham, D. (2009). *Why don't students like school? A cognitive scientist answers questions about how the mind works and what it means for the classroom*. San Francisco: John Wiley and Sons.

Chapter 3
What We Know About the Digital Generation

> There's nothing wrong with the next generation. What's wrong is with our generation and our small mind, small hearts issues—we just buy the illusions.
>
> **Jennifer James, speech to Oregon School Board Association**

Because of constant digital bombardment, the emergence of the new digital landscape, and the pervasive nature of digital experiences, children today are growing up digitally enhanced. Because they have grown up in a digital environment, new research is inferring that the brains of the digital generation have and continue to change physically and chemically—our children and our students are actually neurologically wired differently than our generation (Small & Vorgon, 2008). They have developed a cultural brain (from Doidge, 2007, p. 207). They have developed what we call hypertext/hyperlinked minds. Their cognitive structures process information in a parallel or simultaneous manner, not sequential like ours. Even though we don't yet fully understand the incredibly complex processes involved in thinking and learning, it's important that we take a closer look at what we have recently learned.

First, consider that even today, we know more about outer space than we do about inner space. For example, even though the human brain makes up only 2 percent of body weight, it uses 15 percent to 20 percent of the oxygen consumed (Davis & Buskist, 2008, p. 140).

For what this energy is used, we're still not certain. Furthermore, research tells us that we come into the world with about 50 percent of the brain wiring in place to handle critical initial functions, while the other 50 percent happens after birth (Clarke & Sokoloff, 1999, pp. 637–670).

Growing Up in Our Generation

We know both from the research and from personal experience that learning a first language or even a second language comes easiest to us during our first years of life. However, for most of us, as we get older, learning a second language becomes increasingly difficult. It's not that we can't learn other languages, but when we do, we tend to have more of an accent and often have problems learning one or more aspects of the new language. Learning a language later in life is just not as easy as learning one early on (Singleton & Lengyel, 1995, pp. 30–50).

Let's use this observation as an analogy for what's going on with our children in the new digital landscape from the perspective of their internalization of the digital language.

Children Really Are Different

Recently, there have been several very interesting books on the brain and learning. These include *iBrain* by Gary Small and Gigi Vorgon, *The Brain That Changes Itself* by Norman Doidge, *Everything Bad Is Good for You* by Steven Johnson, *A Whole New Mind* by Daniel Pink, *Brain Rules* by John Medina, and *Grown Up Digital* by Donald Tapscott.

Each in its own way comes to a similar conclusion: that children today are different. In fact, based on the commentary of these writers, it is easy to conclude that children today are fundamentally different in the way they think; the way they access, absorb, interpret, process, and use information; and in the way they view, interact, and communicate in the modern world—and that these differences are due in large part to their experiences with digital technologies. If this is true, it holds profound implications for all of us personally and professionally. Let's examine what we know.

Conventional Wisdom

For the longest time, many neuroscientists believed that different areas of the brain were "hardwired" and stable shortly after birth to handle different aspects of brain function (Clarke & Sokoloff, 1999, pp. 637–670). Conventional thinking was that by the age of 3, the brain was fixed; from that point on, our brains really did not change. By the age of 3, we had a fixed number of brain cells, which then started to die off one by one with no appreciable new cell growth—meaning, in essence, that you really couldn't teach an old dog new tricks.

As a result, the long-standing assumption has been that we all have a fixed memory, fixed processing power, and fixed intelligence—and that the brain we developed by the age of 3 was essentially the same brain we would have at death. This was believed to be the case for all brains regardless of race, culture, or experiences. The assumption was that we all thought in basically the same way because we all used the same neural pathways or neural electronic circuitry to take in, process, and utilize information (Clarke & Sokoloff, 1999, pp. 637–670).

What We Have Learned

However, certain cognitive changes, such as recovery from brain injury or stroke, demonstrate that the brain has the capability to change itself given the right conditions (Doidge, 2007; Small & Vorgon, 2008). Over the past 20 years, because of a number of major scientific and technological breakthroughs, many of these long-standing assumptions have been shown to be completely wrong.

New scanning techniques combined with neuroscience and neurobiological research have demonstrated in one brain area after another and in system after system that, on the contrary, the brain is actually highly adaptive (or "plastic") and remains malleable throughout life.

The old idea that we all have a fixed number of brain cells has been replaced by research showing that our supply of brain cells is continually being replenished—the brain is constantly reorganizing itself structurally throughout life based on two critical factors.

First is the input or experiences we have, and second is the intensity and duration of those experiences (Small & Vorgon, 2008, p. 16).

We know this happens because the research tells us that neural circuits are constantly being strengthened or weakened based on the intensity and duration of the inputs. Brain cells and their circuits operate on a use-it-or-lose-it, survival-of-the-fittest principle (Chechik, Meilijson, & Ruppin, 1999).

What this means in layman's terms is that you can change memory capacity, change neural processing power, regrow neurons, and change neural circuitry throughout your life. As a result, the intelligence we're born with is not fixed.

Measurable intelligence actually rises and falls depending on the type and duration of stimulation to which our brains are exposed, which in itself holds enormous implications ranging from, at one end, being able to enhance cognitive performance to, at the other end, being able to arrest or reverse neural disorders (Neisser, 2003, pp. 67–154).

Neuroplasticity in the Brain

Neuroplasticity is the process of ongoing reorganization and restructuring of the brain in response to intensive inputs and constant stimulation. The result is that the neurons constantly rearrange themselves, making new connections and pruning unnecessary neurons to speed and reroute the flow of thought. The brain is plastic in nature.

Therefore, contrary to long-standing assumptions, the brain restructures neural pathways on an ongoing basis throughout our lives. It makes new cells, creates new connections, sets up new circuitry, and, as a result, constantly creates new thinking patterns.

Recommended Readings

There have been a number of new books written on neuroplasticity and the digital generation. We've included an extensive bibliography in this book, but in particular we would highly recommend three.

The first is Norman Doidge's (2007) book *The Brain That Changes Itself: Stories of Personal Triumph From the Frontiers of Brain Science*. This book explains in clear and simple language exactly what neuroplasticity is and what it implies for learning. It also has a lengthy examination of the cultural brain—what prevailing culture does to neural processes and, in particular, what digital culture and digital bombardment is doing to the digital generation (pp. 287–311).

A second excellent book is *Everything Bad Is Good for You* by Steven Johnson (2005). Johnson says that complex games and new technologies are already educating our kids before and after school. Below our radar they are having a powerful effect on their thinking processes. As a result of digital bombardment, Johnson says, children today arrive in the classroom with a completely different set of cognitive skills and habits than past generations had and that their devices have become extensions of themselves, indispensable social and learning accessories.

Johnson argues that contrary to what the people of our generation might believe, gaming isn't just for slackers. He suggests that gaming and much of today's television offerings can be mentally enriching—they sharpen thinking, hone social skills, and fine-tune perception. Furthermore, he asserts that the plots of today's video games, movies, and television programs challenge young viewers to think like grown-ups, follow intricate narratives, and analyze complex social networks—far more advanced plots and stories than the narratives we experienced when we were growing up—and that these activities are an exercise for the mind the way physical activity exercises the body.

As a result, Johnson suggests that the way gamers explore virtual worlds mirrors the way the brain processes multiple but interconnected streams of information in the real world. He suggests that this generation of learners have become very sophisticated thinkers who, among other things, have learned to take risks without being reckless, have learned to deal with failure, and are confident, motivated, and expect a lot of themselves in areas they care about. These are the minds of children growing up in a nonlinear, light-, and sound-based culture.

The problem is that the many skills digital bombardment has enhanced, such as parallel processing, graphics awareness, and random access (which are sophisticated and valuable thinking skills that have profound implications for learning), are almost totally ignored by educators. Furthermore, they are not generally measured by the current school systems, No Child Left Behind (a.k.a. No Child Left Untested), or the assessments that we use to measure achievement.

As a result, the digital generation, who are accustomed to the twitch-speed, multitasking, random-access, graphics-first, active, connected, fun, fantasy, quick-payoff world of their video games, MTV, and the Internet, are incredibly bored by most of today's education.

In the past few years increasing concern has been expressed about the digital generation's fascination with multitasking, or attending to several things at once. They are completely comfortable with the sense of "highway hypnosis"—the ability to drive or multitask with little memory of the process of getting there.

Human beings have always had the capacity to multitask. Mothers have done it since the hunter-gatherer era—picking berries while suckling an infant, stirring the pot with one eye on the toddler. Electronic multitasking isn't entirely new either—we've been driving while listening to car radios since they became popular in the 1930s. But there is no doubt that the phenomenon has reached a kind of warp speed in the era of web-enabled computers, when it has become routine to conduct six instant messenger conversations, watch American Idol on television, and Google the names of last season's finalists all at once.

That level of multiprocessing and interpersonal connectivity is now so commonplace that it's easy to forget how quickly it came about. Fifteen years ago, most home computers weren't even linked to the Internet. Any number of dire predictions have been made about the long-term effect of multitasking on the digital generation's neural processes, and this is not surprising. Every generation since the time of Socrates, including our parents' generation, has had trouble dealing with their children—it's not that they're deficient, it's that they're different. Every generation of adults sees new technology, and the new thinking behind it and the social changes it stirs, as a threat to the rightful order of things.

Plato warned (correctly) that reading would be the downfall of oral tradition and memory. Ever since then, every generation of teenagers has embraced the freedoms and possibilities wrought by new technologies in ways that shock the elders and break away from the way things traditionally have been done.

Most adults (including the critics) can't play the modern, complex games (and discount the opinions of the kids who do play them). Instead, they rely on secondhand sources of information, most of which are sadly misinformed about both the harm and the true benefits of game playing, because how kids now communicate, how kids read, and how kids choose to interact with information and others doesn't conform with our traditional definition of literacy.

> *. . . gaming and much of today's television offerings can be mentally enriching—they sharpen thinking, hone social skills, and fine-tune perception.*

Another related book is Daniel Pink's (2005) *A Whole New Mind: Moving From the Information Age to the Conceptual Age*. Pink says that we live in a predominantly linear, logical, left to right, top to bottom, beginning to end, left-brain society. The left side of the brain specializes in recognizing serial events like talking, reading, writing, and numeracy. It is particularly good at decoding things that march in single file. It handles logic. It deals in the literalness of meaning. Schools have traditionally focused on left-brain thinking and with good reason. Left-brain thinking was the basis of the incredible success of the Industrial Age.

This left-brained focus is, and long has been, the mindset behind education and testing. Pink notes this emphasis is increasingly educating creativity out of children and that, given the state and rate of change in our society today, if all kids learn to do is read, write, and numerate by 20th-century standards, they will not be literate by the standards of the 21st century.

Pink states that the role of the right side of the brain, which primarily handles pattern analysis, problem solving, big picture thinking, intuition, creativity, connecting the dots, synthesis, emotional expression, context, and putting the big picture together to create meaning by resolving contradiction in order to make sense of situations and to determine significance, has long been undervalued, underappreciated, and misunderstood in our predominantly left-brained society.

Pink then says that almost anything that involves predominantly left-brained thinking will or already has been automated, turned into hardware or software, or outsourced. Of course, we know that the brain's two halves work together as an integrated whole, and that we never use one side of the brain without the other. But what Pink offers is that if our children are going to survive, let alone thrive, in the culture and workplace of the 21st century, they are going to have to move from being linear, logical, left-brain thinkers to whole-brain thinkers. He adds that creativity and problem solving are as important as traditional literacy and memorization, and that we should treat creativity and problem solving with the same status we do traditional literacy. If we're going to do this, education is going to have to provide experiences that require students to use both hemispheres together—we're going to have to educate the "whole new mind."

Qualifying the Research

The caution here is that brains don't just change spontaneously. Our neural circuits may fit a common cerebral architecture, but are molded by our life and learning experiences. For the brain to become neuroplastic requires that there be intensive, sustained, progressively challenging stimulation and focus that happens over extended periods of time. What we're talking about here is several hours a day, seven days a week.

For example, learning to read and write requires that our brains be reprogrammed or rewired over extended periods of time—exposure for several hours a day, seven days a week.

In the same way, watching television for extended periods of time reprograms or rewires our brains. But again, this requires several hours a day, seven days a week (Small & Vorgon, 2008, p. 2).

Does several hours a day, seven days a week remind you of anything else happening in our children's lives today?

The Impact of Video Games and Digital Devices

Since the arrival of Pong in 1974, followed quickly thereafter by SuperPong, Donkey Kong, PacMan, SimCity, and Space Invaders, this is increasingly what's been happening to the digital generation's brains several hours a day, seven days a week. And now it's Madden Football, Grand Theft Auto, Tony Hawk, SimCity, and arcade games.

Today, solo games, which were the norm in the period before computers became networked, have mostly been supplanted by massively multiplayer online role playing games (MMORPGs) like EverQuest, World of Warcraft, Runescape, Maple Story, and virtual learning environments such as Second Life.

Millions of people globally pay to play in three-dimensional game worlds—and it's not unusual for several million people to be online at the same time, playing the same game simultaneously and working collaboratively or competing against one another. These experiences are examples of digital bombardment.

Digital Bombardment

Many children have spent their entire lives surrounded by and using computers, video games, DVD players, cell phones, iPods, and a never-ending list of inexpensive digital wonders. In a recent study undertaken by the Pew Internet, it is estimated that one-half of all 4- to 6-year-old children and three-fourths of teenagers play video games on handheld devices, computers, or consoles several hours a day, several times a week (Lenhart, Madden, Smith, & Macgill, 2007). We need to stop and consider the implications of this constant exposure to digital devices and digital experiences.

The Brain as a Tree

The brain is like a tree. First, there's a flurry of growth—the tree grows extra branches, twigs, and roots. Then the unused branches or pathways are pruned away, and it is this pruning that gives the tree its shape for the future. This is what is meant by "use it or lose it"—the cells and connections that are redundant or seldom used are pruned away, and they wither and die.

As new neuronal connections form during the early part of childhood, heavily used pathways become coated or insulated by myelin, a fatty insulating sheath that speeds signal transmission. Myelin boosts signal transmission speeds in the brain more than 13 times. This is a jump in speed analogous to switching your Internet connection from dial-up to broadband.

Myelinated circuits also transmit 30 times more information per second, giving them not only greater speed but also greater bandwidth. If a student is only attending to music or sports or academics, those are the cells and neural pathways that will become hardwired and insulated.

However, if that same student is lying on the couch playing video games or watching television, those are the cells and connections that are going to flourish. The most useful connections develop into a neural network as a result of regular exposure, or, if the connections are not useful, they're pruned away.

How Have Changes in the Brain Affected the Digital Generation?

As a result, even among today's youngest children, with a multitude of inexpensive digital devices and gadgets that facilitate hypertext, interactivity, networking, random access, and multitasking, digital bombardment is wiring and then rewiring kids' brains on an ongoing basis, particularly enhancing visual memory and visual processing skills. As a result of these digital experiences, some are now beginning to conclude that our students are processing the very same information we process, but differently than we do (Small & Gorgon, 2008; Tapscott, 2009). We know this because of the Human Brain Project (en.wikipedia.org/wiki/Human_Brain_Project).

The Human Brain Project

Research about how the brain and mind function has been going on for several years at universities and research facilities around the world. During this time, a new field of study called neuroinformatics has emerged.

Neuroinformatics involves the digital analysis of brain processes by means of neural scanning and imaging using the incredible number-crunching power of computers and our growing understanding of the chemistry and biology of the brain.

For the first time, using powerful brain scanners and imaging techniques, including functional magnetic resonance imaging (fMRIs), positron emission tomography (PET) scans, and optical topography (OT), we can get inside the black box and examine the functions of normal and impaired living brains noninvasively while they are involved in various cognitive tasks.

If you break a bone, an x-ray will reveal the break that has already taken place. If you tear a ligament, an MRI will show the tear that has taken place. What makes these tests so unique as we study the brain is that an fMRI, for instance, shows the phenomenon as it is happening. The small f in fMRI means "functional"—in "real time" we can give a book to a child who has dyslexia and ask him or her to read as we watch the patterns in the brain.

With these technologies, researchers can digitally view and analyze a living brain's processing patterns at the molecular level in real-time and 3-D to determine what parts of the brain and what specific neural circuitry are being used during specific mental processes.

These technologies allow researchers to be able to pinpoint to within a few millimeters the parts of the brain that "light up" or turn on when people view vivid colors, react to pictures of calorie-rich desserts, stare at pictures of fearful faces, or even simple things such as move a finger, feel sad, add two plus two, or do other specific tasks.

The Brainbow

Recently, another huge leap forward was revealed. Scientists announced the development of a new imaging technology called the Brainbow (Lichtman & Sanes, 2007). The Brainbow allows researchers to color code different neural pathways the same way we color code house wiring to trace electrical pathways back to their source.

The Brainbow will eventually allow researchers to determine the specific neural pathways that are used during specific thought processes. These and many more developments are helping researchers understand how different areas of the brain interact to handle even the simplest of tasks. As a result of these and many other developments, we've probably learned more about how the brain operates and how the mind functions in the last few years than we did in the previous 100 years.

The Effect of Digital Bombardment

Let's consider the effect of digital bombardment on the visual cortex. Consider that the average video game takes about 40 hours to play, and the complexity of the puzzles and objectives grows steadily over time as the game progresses. A study by the University of Rochester found that visual processing dramatically increases with as little as 10 hours of game play (Green & Bavelier, 2005, p.1064).

It goes without saying that these developments hold enormous implications for educators. According to developmental molecular biologist John Medina, in his amazing, hilarious, and informative new book *Brain Rules* (2008, pp. 233–234), tests show that people can remember the content of more than 2,500 pictures with at least 90 percent accuracy 72 hours after exposure even though the subjects see each picture only for about 10 seconds. Recall rates one year later still hovered around 63 percent.

This same research says that if new information is presented orally with no image present, people only remember about 10 percent of what was presented 72 hours after exposure to the images—but the percentage remembered goes up to 65 percent if a picture is added to the new material after the fact. It turns out that the reason for this is that the eye processes and interprets the content of complex imagery, such as photographs, 60,000 times faster than it does words (Burmark, 2002, p. 5).

The reason for this is that the brain is much more suited to processing visual information than anything else because nerve cells devoted to visual processing account for about 30 percent of the brain's cortex, compared to only 8 percent for touch and 3 percent for hearing.

It's completely natural that today's students might be far more inclined toward visual processing than text processing. Do you think that this might hold any implications for the way they learn most effectively? Furthermore, this study says that because the digital generation thinks graphically, their eyes move differently than the eyes of the people of our generation when they scan reading materials.

Changes in Digital Readers

The eyes of older generations unconsciously find an intersection about one-third of the way down the page and one-third of the way in from the left side. This is what the Greeks called the "Golden Mean." Then we read in what's called a Z curve (Holmqvist, K. and Wartenberg, C. (2005). The role of local design factors for newspaper reading behaviour—an eye-tracking perspective. Lund University Cognitive Studies, LUCS 127 ISSN 1101-8453 - page 4)—a complex Z curve if there's lots of information on the page; or a simple Z curve if there's only a small amount of information. (Warlick, D. (2007). F-Patterns and hot spots on web pages. http://www.blackartofwebpublishing.com/FPatternHotSpots)

However, recent research tells us that people consume digital content in a fundamentally different manner than they do traditionally printed physical content. (Nielsen, J. (2006). Jakob Nielsen's Alertbox, April 17, 2006: F-shaped pattern for reading web content. http://www.useit.com/alertbox/reading_pattern.html) The factors, which include text being harder to read and digitally formatted materials inbuilt opportunity to quickly move to other information (links and searching), results in most of digital readers 'scanning' rather than reading digital content. Nielsen's studies show where people's eyes spend the most time and therefore infer the most heavily consumed content. Working with Kent State University, Nielsen developed a series of thermographic prints using a heat map to track eye movement of students in different reading configurations and then summed the records. The brighter the color, the more the reader has focused on the information in that area, and the darker the color, the less the reader had focused on that area.. The images, which can be seen at www.useit.com/alertbox/reading_pattern.html, also illustrate that digital readers read in the F-pattern. (To view of video of F-pattern reading, see http://sethgodin.typepad.com/seths_blog/2006/05/what_i_learned_.html).

Once digital readers have consumed the compelling images and strong colors of a page, their consumption of text content tends towards two horizontal passes and a slow vertical pass creating an F-shape. Different color and dwell settings on eye-tracking equipment turn this 'F' shape into a triangle that points to the top-left corner of the page. Google (and others) call this the 'golden triangle'. (See http://www.blackartofwebpublishing.com/FPatternHotSpots)

Since an increasing amount of information is being delivered in a digital format, it is critical for educators to understand that young readers unconsciously use different very different eye movement patterns when browsing a text-based page than they would to read things presented in a digital format .

The qualification here is that eye-tracking patterns only show us where the eye spends the most time, not the actual path, not what was picked up in peripheral vision and certainly not a measure of the information that 'stuck' in the mind of our visitors. In fact, if you follow the path of the eye, rather than on where the eye dwells, there is a rapid settling movement, followed by anchoring on some strong attention grabbing point and then, once 'eye-grabbing' graphic elements are consumed, the visitor's scanning pattern is actually still pretty much the same Z-pattern that we all use to read printed text (at least English printed text). The difference is scanning speed and our short length of patience with the online media.. As Daniel Ethier recently pointed out to Ian in an email, "The reading pattern seems influenced by what the reader is intending to do (scan, search, read) and the layout of what's being read. People often seem to scan online text, deciding whether it's worth a read. People tend to scan the online news. I think you can safely say that people read different media differently based on layout and their intent. The tools do give web publishers the ability to test whether students or others are paying attention to things or getting confused by things, and that is valuable and exciting. That seems to be the intent of the Kent State work.

As Jakob Nielsen points out (Nielsen, J. (2006). Jakob Nielsen's Alertbox, April 17, 2006: F-shaped pattern for reading web content. http://www.useit.com/alertbox/reading_pattern.html) the implications of F pattern reading are that digital readers won't read text thoroughly in a word-by-word manner. Exhaustive reading is rare. Some people will read more, but most won't. The first two paragraphs must state the most important information. There's some hope that users will actually read this material, though they'll probably read more of the first paragraph than the second. Subheads, paragraphs, and bullet points must with information-carrying words that users will notice when scanning down the left side of the content in the final stem of their F-behavior. It's fascinating to watch the slow-motion replay of users' eye movements as they read and scan across a page. Every page has reading issues beyond the dominant F pattern being discussed here.

However the bottom line is that digital bombardment has changed reading patterns. Increasingly digital readers tend to unconsciously ignore the right side and bottom half of the page and tend to only read content in those areas if they are highly motivated to do so. One has to wonder if this trend holds any implications for designing engaging reading materials for a generation that increasingly expect to be able to read their information in a digital form?

These findings become even more significant because, according to respected writer Eric Jensen (2008) and others, at least 60 percent of students in any given classroom are not auditory or text-based learners. Increasingly, because of digital bombardment, because they think graphically, and because they've grown up in the new digital landscape, they're either visual or visual kinesthetic learners, or a combination of the two (p. 97).

They're visual and/or kinesthetic not because they're trying to drive us crazy, but because they've been wired that way in the new digital landscape. They're a digital generation wired for multimedia. Yet, as we all know, despite the fact that at least 60 percent of learners are either visual or visual kinesthetic, the vast majority of questions on state exams continue to be based primarily on text or declarative knowledge.

> *Why in the world do I have to remember this when I can Google the answer in three seconds on my cell phone?*

What Does the Research Mean?

According to Prensky (2006), by the time they're 21, the digital generation will have played more than 10,000 hours of video games, sent and received 250,000 emails and text/instant messages, spent 10,000 hours talking on phones, and watched more than 20,000 hours of television and 500,000 commercials (and most assuredly these estimates are on the extreme low side). Almost none of these are experiences our parents or we had while we were growing up (Prensky, 2006, p. 28). Prensky also points out that, at the same time, the digital generation will have spent much less than this amount of time attending school and only about 4,300 hours reading (p. 226).

Beyond this, much of their time is spent unengaged or under engaged. Do you think these experiences and this digital bombardment might have any impact on the way they think, learn, and view the world, or on what engages them?

Our Conclusion

We all process information in slightly different ways based on gender, age, culture and experiences. But with the experiences and stimulation our children have been exposed to, what we are now beginning to understand is that the digital generation processes information differently than the people of our generation. We don't know if you've noticed, but we certainly have—there appears to be an accelerating gap between the mental processing of the younger generations—between the mental processing speed and techniques of teenagers, tweenagers, and younger children. Understanding this helps explain, at least in part, why children are different, why they act the way they do, and why they view the world the way they do. And it also helps to explain some of the fundamental differences between their generation and ours.

Despite the fact that there are more than 40 years of solid research on how learners learn best, how the brain functions, and which instructional practices are the most effective, this research has not been widely accepted or integrated into most classrooms to better help today's learners and their learning and communication preferences. Nor is it reflected in many of the assumptions that are the foundations of public education today.

This is what is frustrating us! So, we just have to ask: If teachers continue to do things in the classroom that we already know don't work, then who here really has the learning problem? Is it the kids, or is it us? The definition of insanity is doing things the same way we've always done, but expecting, wanting, or needing completely different results. If we continue to teach the same way, we will continue to get the same results. And in doing so, we will fail our children.

We hear complaints all the time that kids today can't concentrate or that kids can't even memorize the names of the states and their capitals. Many kids are increasingly saying, "Why in the world do I have to remember this when I can Google the answer in three seconds on my cell phone?" Meanwhile, many teachers are saying, "What's a Google?"

These same kids who can't remember the names of the states and their capitals can instantly and with enthusiasm tell you the lyrics of 1,000 songs or the characteristics of 100 game characters. It's not that most of these kids have ADD or ADHD, and it's not that they're disabled; it's that they're bored, just not interested, just not listening, and increasingly tuning us out. They have no patience for old ways of teaching and learning. The fact that they have no patience should not be surprising. Adults have no more patience for non-engaging materials than kids have, and they have no hesitation in making that known. The problem is that many educators just don't get it. They don't understand how different kids are today—and the digital generation is not just a little different, they're completely different.

And as we said earlier, today's learners are not the same learners that schools were originally designed for, and today's learners are certainly not the learners that many of today's educators were trained to teach. They are different and, as a result, we are increasingly trying to fit round pegs into square holes, and using standardized tests to measure non-standardized brains. The starting point is that we must reconsider how to reshape at least a part of the current classroom learning experience—the way we teach, the way students learn, and the way we assess that learning—and start to address the digital learning styles and learning preferences of the digital generation.

So now we have a pretty good picture of the gap between the adults in control of the school system, who grew up in a predominantly nondigital world, and the digital kids who are growing up in a radically different world that includes the rapidly evolving online digital world. Now that we have described both sides of this gap, it becomes clear that this gap is really more like a huge gulf. Kids today are living a substantially different life than anything we have ever seen before.

This idea that young people are different began to surface in the late 1990s with comments from some parents and teachers. In the few short years since then, the notion that kids are different has progressed from subjective observations to objective research that confirms the early suspicions. As we have just outlined, there are now empirical studies from reputable sources that document the startling changes the digital experience has had on the way young minds operate. This has had a significant impact on the way young people learn that we will explore more fully in the next chapter.

Summarizing the Main Points

- There is a rapidly growing gap of understanding between the young people sitting in classrooms and the adults who teach them and make decisions about what they will learn, where they will learn, and how they will learn.

- Connecting with students is a key to effective teaching.

- Because of our own experiences growing up, we have a problem letting go of our past assumptions about teaching and learning.

- The world young people experience today is a very different place than the one we grew up in.

- Our students are the digital generation, and our generations are primarily nondigitally oriented.

- In the past few years, we have learned a great deal about how the brain and mind function.

- Neuroplasticity is the reason for the ongoing reorganization and restructuring of the brain in response to intensive inputs and constant stimulation.

- Video games, assorted digital devices, and digital bombardment have had a profound effect on the digital generation.

- A new field of study called neuroinformatics has emerged during the past several years.

- Digital bombardment is having a powerful effect on the way the digital generation processes information.

- More than 60 percent of students are either visual or visual kinesthetic learners.

- The digital generation processes information differently than the people of our generation, and there appears to be a growing gap between the younger generations.

Some Questions to Consider

- How are our students the same or different than they were 20 years ago?
- How are our teachers the same or different than they were 20 years ago?
- How are classrooms the same or different than they were 20 years ago?
- What are the next steps I need to take to begin to move from where I am to where I think I need to be?
- What message do parents and community members need to hear?
- What message do the school board and district management need to hear?

Reading and References

Burmark, L. (2002). *Visual literacy: Learn to see, see to learn*. New York: ASCD.

Buskist, W., & Davis, W., (2008). *Handbook of the teaching of psychology*. Malden, MA: Blackwell Publishing.

Byerly, G., Holmes, J., Robins, D., Zang, Y., & Salaba, A., (2006). *The "eyes" have it—Eye-tracking and usability study of schoolrooms*. SirsiDynix OneSource June 2006   VOLUME 2 ISSUE 6: Kent State University School of Library and Information Science.

Canton, J. (2006). *The extreme future: The top trends that will reshape the world for the next 5, 10, and 20 years*. New York: Penguin.

Carter, R. (2009). *The human brain book: An illustrated guide to its structure, function, and disorders*. London: Dorling Kindersley.

Chechik, G., Meilijson, I., & Ruppin, E., (1999). *Neuronal Regulation: A Mechanism for Synaptic Pruning During Brain Maturation. (Volume 11, Issue 8.)* Cambridge, MA: MIT Press.

Clarke, D. D., & Sokoloff L. (1999). Imagining techniques for the localization of brain function. In Stephen F. Davis, & William Buskist (Ed.), *21st Century Psychology: A Reference Handbook*, p.148. Thousand Oaks, CA: Sage.

Doidge, N. (2007). *The brain that changes itself: Stories of personal triumph from the frontiers of brain scien*ce. New York: Penguin.

Feinstein, S. (2004). *Secrets of the teenage brain: Research-based strategies for reaching and teaching today's adolescents*. San Diego, CA: The Brain Store.

Green, S., & Bavelier, D. (2005, September). Effects of video game playing on visual processing across space. *Journal of Vision*, 5(8).

Holmqvist, K. and Wartenberg, C. (2005). *The role of local design factors for newspaper reading behaviour—an eye-tracking perspective*. Lund University Cognitive Studies, LUCS 127 ISSN 1101-8453

Johnson, S. (2005). *Everything bad is good for you: How today's popular culture is actually making us smarter*. New York: Riverhead.

Jensen, E., (2008). Super Teaching: Over 1000 Practical Strategies. p. 42. Thousand Oaks, CA: Corwin Press.

Kurzweil, R. (2005). *The singularity is near: When humans transcend biology*. New York: Viking Press.

Lenhart, A., Madden, M., Smith, A., & Macgill, A. (2007). *Teens and Social Media*. Washington, DC: Pew Research Center's Internet & American Life Project.

Longstaff, H. (1949). *Review of attention and interest factors in advertising*. Journal of Applied Psychology. Vol 33(3), Jun 1949, pages 286-287.

Medina, J. (2008). *Brain rules: 12 principles for surviving and thriving at work, home, and school*. Seattle, WA: Pear Press.

Nielsen, J. (2006). Jakob Nielsen's Alertbox, April 17, 2006: *F-shaped pattern for reading web content*. http://www.useit.com/alertbox/reading_pattern.html

Nielsen, J. and Loranger, H. (2006). *Prioritizing web usability*. Berkley: New Riders Press

Nielson, J. and Pernice, K. (2010). *Eyetracking web usability*. Berkley: New Riders Press

Neisser, U., & Hyman, Y. (1999). *Memory Observed: Remembering in Natural Contexts*. (2nd Edition). New York: Worth Publishing.

Nussbaum, P., & Daggett, W. (2008). *What brain research teaches us about rigor, relevance, and relationships—And what it teaches us about keeping your own brain healthy*. Rexford, NY: International Center for Leadership in Education.

Penn, W. (1956). *Research in marketing*.The Journal of Marketing, Vol. 21, No. 2 pages 200-228. American Marketing Association. http://www.jstor.org/stable/1247344

Pink, D. (2005). *A whole new mind: Moving from the information age to the conceptual age*. New York: Riverhead.

Poole, A., Ball, L. J., and Phillips, P. (2004). *In search of salience: A response time and eye movement analysis of bookmark recognition*. In S. Fincher, P. Markopolous, D. Moore, & R. Ruddle (Eds.), People and Computers XVIII-Design for Life: Proceedings of HCI 2004. London: Springer-Verlag Ltd.

Prensky, M. (2006). *Don't bother me mom—I'm learning*. p. 28, 226. St. Paul, MN: Paragon House.

Rayner, K. (1998). *Eye movements in reading and information processing: 20 years of research*. Psychological Bulletin, 124, 372-422.

Sexton, J. (2009). *Doesn't graphic design/layout affect scanning patterns?—* http://www.grokdotcom.com/2009/04/08/doesnt-graphic-designlayout-affect-scanning-patterns/

Singleton, D., & Lengyl, Z. (1995). *The Age Factor in Second Language Acquisition*. Bristol, UK: Multilingual Matters Ltd.

Small, G., & Vorgon, G. (2008). *iBrain: Surviving the technological alteration of the modern mind*. New York: Harper Collins.

Tapscott, D. (2009). *Grown up digital: How the net generation is changing your world*. New York: McGraw-Hill.

Vangeliakos, C., (2007). *Neuroscience researchers expand usage of brainbow technology*. www.thecrimson.com/article/2007/11/2/neuroscience-researchers-expand-usage-of-brainbow/ Cambridge MA: Harvard Crimson.

Warlick, D. (2007). *F-Patterns and hot spots on web pages—* http://www.blackartofwebpublishing.com/FPatternHotSpots

Willingham, D. (2009). *Why don't students like school? A cognitive scientist answers questions about how the mind works and what it means for the classroom*. San Francisco: John Wiley and Sons.

Zittrain, J. (2008). *The future of the Internet—And how to stop it*. New York: Yale University Press.

Chapter 4
Learning Preferences of the Digital Generation

> Our educational system is running like a fine Swiss watch. The problem is that there is very little market today for fine Swiss watches.
>
> **David Thornburg**

We have outlined some important differences in the way kids today are getting and processing information as compared to the way their parents and teachers do. From the work of writers such as Prensky, Pink, Johnson, Tapscott, Medina, and many others, let's summarize some of the key aspects of how the digital generation learns. You'll see these in the following table alongside the teaching preference of the vast majority of traditional teachers.

Digital Learners Prefer	Many Educators Prefer
Receiving information quickly from multiple multimedia sources	Slow and controlled release of information from limited sources
Processing pictures, sounds, color, and video before text	To provide text before pictures, sounds, color, and video
Random access to hyperlinked multimedia information	To provide information linearly, logically, and sequentially
To network simultaneously with many others	Students to work independently before they network and interact
Learning "just in time"	Teaching "just in case"
Instant gratification with immediate and deferred rewards	Deferred gratification and delayed rewards
Learning that is relevant, active, instantly useful, and fun	Teaching memorization in preparation for standardized tests

Let's take a closer look at what each one of these differences means.

Digital learners prefer receiving information quickly from multiple multimedia sources.	Many educators prefer slow and controlled release of information from limited sources.

Today's generations operate at twitch speed due to constant exposure to video games, cell phones, handheld devices, hypertext, and all of the other experiences that reflect an increasingly digital world, together with an expectation that they will have access to this world. As a result, digital learners have had far more experience at processing information quickly than our generations have, and they're better at dealing with high-speed information. To borrow a phrase from the movie "Top Gun," digital learners have "a need for speed."

But many teachers haven't had those experiences and only feel comfortable processing information at the conventional speed they have experienced most of their lives. As a result, after spending hours of their lives playing video games, talking on cell phones, using digital devices, surfing the Web, and wandering around in virtual worlds, many digital learners run into a wall when they come to school and are forced to slow it down or dumb it down in order to function.

If we are really going to connect to this generation, we need to be willing, at least some of the time, to acknowledge and embrace in classrooms the digital world that's an everyday and internalized part of students' lives outside of school.

And no less an authority than the National School Board Association (NSBA) has recently released a report (Creating & Connecting—Research Guidelines on Social and Educational Networking, 2008) that says by ignoring technologies and global trends that are happening outside of schools and by banning from our classrooms the digital tools and resources that are an everyday part of the lives of young and old alike, whether at work or at play, without first considering the educational possibilities, we are absolutely *blowing* an opportunity to connect with and engage the digital generation—and we are losing them. The NSBA's message to educators is that the world has changed, and it's time for us to acknowledge this, to get over it, and to get on with adequately preparing our students for the world that awaits them when they leave school.

From the earliest times, we've always been able to multitask. This is called continuous partial attention and involves randomly toggling between tasks, deciding which one to do next. For example, we can be driving in the car, listening to music, sipping on some water, reflecting about what happened at work today, checking the rearview mirror, talking on a cell phone, planning dinner, and thinking about things that need to be done. But with the digital generation in our increasingly digital world, this stuff all happens faster.

What the research says is that effective multitasking is really about having a good memory capable of paying attention to several inputs at one time and being highly adept at task switching—but this isn't the way we grew up.

Many of us can personally remember our parents coming into our bedroom and telling us to turn off the radio because we were supposed to be studying. Ian remembers being told by teachers that the best way to study was to isolate himself from the television, the tape player, and the busy sidewalks outside the window. He was told to clear a nice study corner, with a comfy chair, good lighting, and ample workspace.

Contrast that with the ways things are these days. Just walk into a student's bedroom today. There they are, working at a computer, iPod earbuds dangling around their neck cranking out some band we've never heard of, hand reflexively tapping the backbeat, doing their homework, downloading music, burning a DVD, searching for something online, and chatting on six IM screens while simultaneously carrying on two conversations on MySpace about last night's American Idol with the window behind that holding an old Pong game paused mid-ping—and they're still bored. And if you ask them, they will tell you that playing the music loud *helps* them concentrate.

Digital learners prefer processing pictures, sounds, color, and video before text.	Many educators prefer to provide text before pictures, sounds, color, and video.

For generations, graphics were generally static illustrations, photos, or diagrams that accompanied the text and provided some kind of clarification to a concept. For example, many people of our generation remember reading the paper-based *Encyclopedia Britannica* or the *Book of Knowledge*. Back then, the primary information was provided by the text, and the images were intended to complement the text.

For the digital generation, the relationship is almost completely reversed. The role of text is to provide more detail to something that was first experienced as an image or a video.

Since childhood, the digital generation has been continuously exposed to television, videos, the Internet, and computer games that put colorful, high-quality, highly expressive graphics in front of them with little or no accompanying text. The result of this experience has been to considerably sharpen their visual abilities. They find it much more natural than our generation to begin with visuals and to mix text and graphics in richly meaningful and personal ways. It is just as important for digital learners to be taught to communicate with graphics as it is to communicate with text. Visual fluency needs to be embedded into every subject and every grade level and needs to be the responsibility of every teacher from kindergarten to post-secondary.

Digital learners prefer random access to hyperlinked multimedia information.	Many teachers prefer to provide information linearly, logically, and sequentially.

Buckminster Fuller (2008) once wrote, "How often I saw where I should be going by setting out for somewhere else." The under-30 generation is the first to experience hypertext and "clicking around" in children's computer applications, in DVD-ROMs, in video games, and on the Web. This new information structure has increased their awareness and ability to make connections and has freed them from the traditional paper-based constraints of a single path of thought. In our humble opinion, this is generally an extremely positive development.

At the same time, it can be argued with some justification that unlimited hyperlinking may make it more difficult for some students to follow a linear train of thought and to do some types of deep or logical thinking because they become easily bored or distracted.

For digital learners, their mindset goes something like, "Why should I read something from beginning to end, or follow someone else's logic, when I can just 'explore the links' and create my own?" While following one's own path often leads to interesting results, understanding someone else's logic is also very important. While the Internet may be far superior for quickly finding related bits of information or for understanding a topic deeply, it still requires the ability for extended focus and reflection.

What has to be made clear to digital learners and educators alike is that this is not a matter of either/or, us or them, my way or wrong way. Both sets of skills—both traditional and digital, both linear and nonlinear learning styles—are equally essential today.

> Digital learners prefer to network simultaneously with many others.

> Many educators prefer students to work independently before they network and interact.

When we were students, we were expected, at least in the beginning when new information was being introduced, to work independently. When we were out of school, the only ways we were really able to communicate with others was either face-to-face or by phone. Compare this to the digital world of today. The digital generation has grown up with literally dozens and perhaps even hundreds of ways to communicate—cell phones, MySpace, email, texting, blogs, YouTube, Twitter, wikis, and so much more. Since many of these tools have been there for their entire lives, the digital generation have completely internalized their use and take them for granted. Consequently, they need, want, and expect to be able to instantly and seamlessly communicate with others using tools of personal and mass collaboration—and they take for granted that this kind of access to others will be available 24/7. For example, have you ever given someone from the digital generation a new game or device as a gift? A question—what's the first thing they do? Do they pull out the manual and read it like we do? Absolutely not! In the time it takes us to read through the table of contents, they've messed with the new device and already figured out 10 things that work and 10 that don't. Then they go to the Internet and look for blogs, wikis, and message boards for cheats, or they text their buddies to figure out what else they can do.

Let's be clear that this is a fundamentally different kind of learning based on intuition, experimentation, and discovery. This is learning that engages and motivates them. Why would we deny them these kinds of opportunities in the classroom?

> Digital learners prefer learning "just in time."

> Many educators prefer teaching "just in case."

Schools are organized around "just in case." Just in case it's on the exam. Just in case you need to know something to pass the course. Just in case you want to become a scientist or an astronaut. Digital learners prefer to learn just in time. They want an understanding of the things they need to know in order to acquire the necessary skills and knowledge to do something they don't know how to do. Just in time to play a new game, to play that new song on a piano, or to fix a mountain bike. Let's be clear that just-in-time learning is a completely different skill set than just-in-case learning. Just-in-time learning is about having the skills, knowledge, and habits of mind that will allow them to continuously learn and adapt just in time, when that next window of opportunity or area of interest briefly opens to them.

In talking with others, it seems clear that most of us had parents who worked for the same company or worked in the same industry for their entire working career because back then, it was common for someone to spend their entire working lifetime at a single career. Things are different today in the new and constantly changing economy. The idea of having a single career for life is very uncommon. Just look at what has happened to the economy in the past few years. Unemployment is through the roof.

In *The World Is Flat* (2007), Thomas Friedman says that today's generation of students should anticipate having multiple careers in industries that don't yet exist, using technologies that haven't been invented to solve problems we haven't even begun to think about yet. Preparing them for the world that awaits them after school requires a fundamentally different set of skills and knowledge than the skills and knowledge students traditionally leave school with today.

But today, in the age of No Child Left Behind, the problem is that schools continue to be organized around the just-in-case model of teaching and learning. As we pointed out previously, the message to students is that they have to learn this information just in case it might be on the test, or just in case it might be needed to pass the course. So which world are we preparing them for? Are we preparing them for their world or our world?

> Digital learners prefer instant gratification with immediate and deferred rewards.

> Many educators prefer deferred gratification and delayed rewards.

The key here is that the digital world offers a direct connection between the effort expended and the reward received. On the other hand, many of the rewards that are offered by teachers are either too nebulous or too far into the future to motivate students to work for them right now. Teachers tell students that if they study hard, if they keep focused, and if they behave, they might eventually get rewarded with a good letter grade, acceptance to a good school, or the chance for a good job. And we'll be the first to say that it's absolutely essential for students to have this kind of mental focus and discipline—these are absolutely essential skills. The problem is that often these rewards are too distant and have no real meaning in the current lives of students.

A direct connection between effort and reward, immediate or deferred, is why digital culture resonates so strongly with the digital generation. In terms of immediate rewards, digital culture provides them with exactly what they not only want, but what they need most—positive feedback.

Consider how often the digital generation is expected to make decisions while gaming. Recently Ian had a private dinner with a well-known and highly respected video game developer. The developer said that when they design the games, they are organized so that the player has to make a decision every one-half to one second, and that they are rewarded for those efforts every seven to ten seconds. He then suggested we compare that with how often students are asked to make a decision or are positively rewarded in schools. He said that according to his research, students on average got to ask a question or make a personal decision about once every 25 minutes. This may be one of the reasons that many students are waiting for a video game or Internet version of school to come out so they won't have to attend anymore.

However, it is not just immediate feedback that captures the attention of the digital generation. Contrary to what many adults believe, many digital games require players to work hard at frustratingly difficult tasks that can take a considerable amount of time to complete. Young people today will spend hours, days, weeks, or even months trying to master computer games and other digital tools.

In his book, *Everything Bad Is Good for You*, Steven Johnson (2005) points out that young people have not lost the concentration and determination of their parents. They are completely capable of dedicated, tireless effort to succeed at a digital task. Cell phones, social networking tools, digital technology, and video games tell the user that if they put in the hours and if they master the game or the tool, they will be rewarded with the next level, a win, a place on the high scorers' list, or a skill that is respected by their peers. What they do determines exactly what they get, and what they get is clearly worth the hours and hours of effort they have to put in to get there. The reward has meaning in their life right now, and so there is a direct connection between the effort required and the reward received.

> Digital learners prefer learning that is relevant, active, instantly useful, and fun.

> Many educators prefer teaching memorization in preparation for standardized tests.

Many educators feel compelled to teach memorization of the primarily content-based material in the curriculum guide in preparation for the standardized tests they and their students will have to face rather than cultivating higher-order thinking skills—the new and different 21st-century fluency skills these students will need once they leave school.

The digital generation is often derided in the press as being intellectual slackers, disrespectful, and lacking essential social skills. In reality the digital generation is very much an intellectual problem-solving generation. Many types of logic, challenging puzzles, spatial relationships, and other complex thinking tasks are built into the computers and video games they enjoy. And while some "experts" may argue that the experiences the digital generation have are worthless—and that play and games are simply preparation for work and life after school, for today's digital generation, play is work, and work is increasingly seen in terms of games and game play. That's why the digital generation wants their learning to be relevant and instantly useful, and more than anything else, they want to know what possible connections this has to them and their world. And they don't see why this can't be fun most of the time.

Sadly, very little of what we've learned about how our brains and minds function is being applied in the classroom today. Teachers have not been provided with the training needed to incorporate what we have learned about the brains of the digital generation in their classrooms. It is critical that this be addressed immediately because of the huge gap between the digital learning styles and preferences of students today and teachers' nondigital perspectives about teaching, learning, and assessment. Today's children are experiencing a digital world that is increasingly, and some even say completely, out of sync with traditional approaches and assumptions about teaching, learning, and assessment. Despite our best of intentions to do what is right for the digital generation, we are not connecting with modern students mainly because our instruction is targeted at students from another age.

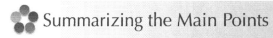

Summarizing the Main Points

- Digital learners prefer receiving information quickly from multiple multimedia sources. Many educators prefer slow and controlled release of information from limited sources.

- Digital learners prefer processing pictures, sounds, color, and video before text. Many educators prefer to provide text before pictures, sounds, color, and video.

- Digital learners prefer random access to hyperlinked multimedia information. Many teachers prefer to provide information linearly, logically, and sequentially.

- Digital learners prefer to network simultaneously with many others. Many educators prefer students to work independently before they network and interact.

- Digital learners prefer learning "just in time." Many educators prefer teaching "just in case."

- Digital learners prefer instant gratification and immediate rewards. Many educators prefer deferred gratification and delayed rewards.

- Digital learners prefer learning that is relevant, active, instantly useful, and fun. Many educators prefer teaching memorization in preparation for standardized tests.

Some Questions to Consider

- What are some of the ways that digital learners are different from learners 20 years ago?

- What differentiated strategies can teachers use to focus more on individuals rather than the entire class?

- By understanding the digital generation's preferences, what different teaching, learning, and assessment strategies can teachers use to move from the traditional stand-and-deliver model of instruction to being the facilitators of learning?

- How can new technologies be used to enhance student learning?

- How can teachers use new technologies to enhance teaching and learning?

Reading and References

Bauerlein, M. (2008). *The dumbest generation: How the digital age stupefies young americans and jeopardizes our future (Or, don't trust anyone under 30).* New York: Tarcher.

Carter, R. (2009). *The human brain book: An illustrated guide to its structure, function, and disorders.* London: Dorling Kindersley.

Christensen, C., Horn, M., & Johnson, C. (2008). *Disrupting class: How disruptive innovation will change the way the world learns.* New York: McGraw-Hill.

Dryden, G., & Vos, J. (2009). *Unlimited: The new learning revolution and the seven keys to unlock it.* Auckland, New Zealand: The Learning Web.

Feinstein, S. (2004). *Secrets of the teenage brain: Research-based strategies for reaching and teaching today's adolescents.* San Diego, CA: The Brain Store.

Friedman, T. (2007). *The world is flat: A brief history of the twenty-first century.* New York: Farrar, Straus and Giroux.

Fuller, B. (2008) *Operating Manual For Spaceship Earth.* p. 16. Baden, Switzerland: Lars Müller Publishers.

Gardner, H. (1983). *Frames of mind: Theories of multiple intelligences.* New York: Basic Books.

Goodstein, A. (2007). *Totally wired: What teens and tweens are really doing online.* New York: St. Martin's Griffin.

Hutchison, D. (2007). *Playing to learn: Video games in the classroom.* Westport, CT: Teacher Ideas Press.

Johnson, S. (2005). *Everything bad is good for you: How today's popular culture is actually making us smarter.* New York: Riverhead.

Kolb, L. (2008). *Toys to tools: Connecting student cell phones to education.* Eugene, OR: ISTE.

McCain, T., & Jukes, I. (2000). *Windows on the future: Education in the age of technology.* Thousand Oaks, CA: Corwin.

Medina, J. (2008). *Brain rules: 12 principles for surviving and thriving at work, home, and school.* Seattle, WA: Pear Press.

National School Board Association. (2007). *Creating and connecting—Research and guidelines on online social and educational networking.* http://www.nsba.org/site/docs/41400/41340.pdf. Alexandria, VA.

Nussbaum, P., & Daggett, W. (2008). *What brain research teaches us about rigor, relevance, and relationships—And what it teaches us about keeping your own brain healthy.* Rexford, NY: International Center for Leadership in Education.

Pink, D. (2005). *A whole new mind: Moving from the information age to the conceptual age.* New York: Riverhead.

Ratey, J., & Hagerman, H. (2008). *Spark: The revolutionary new science of exercise and the brain.* New York: Little, Brown and Company.

Richardson, W. (2008), *Blogs, wikis, podcasts, and other powerful web tools for classrooms.* Thousand Oaks, CA: Corwin.

Small, G., & Vorgon, G. (2008). *iBrain: Surviving the technological alteration of the modern mind.* New York: Harper Collins.

Tapscott, D. (2009). *Grown up digital: How the net generation is changing your world*. New York: McGraw-Hill.

Willingham, D. (2009). *Why don't students like school? A cognitive scientist answers questions about how the mind works and what it means for the classroom*. San Francisco: John Wiley and Sons.

Part II

How Should Education Respond?

Chapter 5
An Impending Tragedy

> For more than 100 years much complaint has been made of the unmethodical way in which schools are conducted, but it is only within the last 30 that any serious attempt has been made to find a remedy for this state of things and with what results? Schools remain exactly as they were.
>
> **Comenius, 1632**

A Growing Disconnect for the Digital Generation

The side-by-side comparison at the beginning of the previous chapter that summarizes the differences between the learning preferences of digital learners and their nondigital teachers is a startling illustration of the huge gulf that has developed in our schools. And it is an absolute recipe for disaster.

If we continue to teach the same old way, we will completely miss connecting with our students. This will not occur because we don't have good things to say, but because we don't know how to say them in a way that students can relate to. Our instruction is targeted at students from another age. We now have a generation that is experiencing a digital world that is out of sync with traditional approaches to teaching.

This disconnect with students is not just happening in the classrooms of older teachers. Younger teachers are also having difficulties because they have spent so much time in institutions based on 20th-century thinking. In their entire time as a student, both in K–12 schools and in universities, they were consistently exposed to the traditional, full-frontal, lecture-style teaching. With very few exceptions, this is the only kind of instruction that was modeled for them, and it forms their context for what teaching looks like. Beyond this, the teacher training most young teachers receive is still based on the traditional approaches developed in the last century that do not adequately address the learning preferences of digital students. While new teachers are encouraged to use technology, the underlying approach to instruction remains largely unchanged.

Consequently, most teachers continue to speak digital as a second language (DSL) when they teach. The students in their classrooms immediately pick up their teachers' nondigital accent and tune them out. This makes it difficult for students to remain engaged in the activities in the classroom.

Many students are leaving the school system altogether. Today in the United States, more than one-third of students and almost one-half of minorities drop out before they complete high school. In Canada, the dropout rate is one in four. Many more of those who do graduate are learning disabled or delayed. What's more, they're increasingly turned off.

According to a recent study, only 28 percent of 12th-grade students believe that schoolwork is meaningful; 21 percent believe that their courses are interesting; and a mere 39 percent believe that schoolwork will have any bearing on their success in later life (National Center for Education Statistics, 2002). These statistics are even more shocking when one realizes that these are only the opinions of those students who have remained in high school for four years. Students who have found the high school experience the least relevant have already exited the system in huge numbers.

An Impending Tragedy for Education

This disconnect between students and the school system is a very real and rapidly growing tragedy for education because educators have much of value to teach young people today. There is much to be gained for our students as we pass on the accumulated knowledge and wisdom of human society in their public education. The knowledge gained in studying the content of the subjects offered in school enables students to understand the increasingly complex world of the 21st century. In addition, the higher-order thinking skills that can be developed while completing the tasks given by teachers empower young people to assess the vast amounts of readily available information to determine its significance for use in solving problems in modern society. Young people miss out on an incredibly valuable experience if they drop out or tune out of school before they have finished.

But there's more. Teachers have some very important cognitive skills to teach young people that are critical for success in the very digital world students live in. There are some large gaps in the learning of digital students. Kids today have impressive skills with technology. For instance, they can download music, play games, rapidly retrieve information from search engines, quickly assess the message in visual media, and communicate using a multitude of wireless and online tools. But the focus of most of these activities is for personal recreational purposes. Use of digital tools for work is often overlooked. The principles behind effective communication in a visual environment are not widely known by young people. The cognitive skills required to solve complex problems using the digital tools they know so well are often underdeveloped.

It would be a tragedy of enormous magnitude if public educators failed to reach their clientele, the digital generation, because we have so much of incredible value to share with them. The heartbreak would be even greater if that failure to reach students resulted from a resistance to change on the part of teachers and administrators. It is a professional imperative that everyone involved in education put aside their own personal preferences for teaching and consider the learning styles of these new students who have grown up in a radically different digital world. If we do not, there is a very real possibility that public education will become increasingly irrelevant to the digital generation. This would be a very sad situation indeed! So with this in mind, we want to outline a number of major changes educators must make to effectively communicate with the digital generation and to adequately prepare them for the wild and exciting technological world of the 21st century.

Summarizing the Main Points

- There is a huge gulf between the learning preferences of digital learners and their nondigital teachers.

- Younger teachers are also having difficulties because they have spent so much time in institutions based on 20th-century thinking and were consistently exposed to the traditional, full-frontal, lecture-style teaching.

- Dropout rates tell us that more than one-third of students and almost one-half of minorities drop out before they complete high school.

- Young people miss out on an incredibly valuable experience if they drop out or tune out of school before they have finished.

- It's time for everyone involved in education to put aside their own personal preferences for teaching and consider the learning styles of these new students who have grown up in a radically different digital world.

 Some Questions to Consider

- How do we address the dropout rate? What do we need to be doing differently?

- What are some of the skills and knowledge above and beyond being able to do well on a bubble test that all students need to operate in the 21st century?

- What strategies can educators use to better engage students in the learning process?

- How can we use the digital generation's interest in new technologies to better support teaching, learning, and assessment of that learning?

- How can we better engage parents and the community in the process of making schools more relevant for students?

Reading and References

Christensen, C., Horn, M., & Johnson, C. (2008). *Disrupting class: How disruptive innovation will change the way the world learns*. New York: McGraw-Hill.

Dryden, G., & Vos, J. (2009). *Unlimited: The new learning revolution and the seven keys to unlock it*. Auckland, New Zealand: The Learning Web.

Friedman, T. (2005). *The world is flat: A brief history of the twenty-first century*. New York: Farrar, Straus and Giroux.

National Center for Education Statistics. (2002). *The Condition of Education 2002*. Washington, DC: U.S. Department of Education.

Pink, D. (2005). *A whole new mind: Moving from the information age to the conceptual age*. New York: Riverhead.

Small, G., & Vorgon, G. (2008). *iBrain: Surviving the technological alteration of the modern mind*. New York: Harper-Collins.

Tapscott, D. (2009). *Grown up digital: How the net generation is changing your world*. New York: McGraw-Hill.

Trilling, B., & Fadel, C. (2009). *21st century skills: Learning for life in our times*. San Francisco: Jossey-Bass.

Wagner, T. (2008). *The global achievement gap: Why even our best schools don't teach the new survival skills our children need and what we can do about it*. New York: Basic Books.

Willingham, D. (2009). *Why don't students like school? A cognitive scientist answers questions about how the mind works and what it means for the classroom*. San Francisco: John Wiley and Sons.

Chapter 6

It's Time to Catch Up

> The principle goal of education is to create men and women who are capable of doing new things, not simply of repeating what other generations have done. Men and women who are creative, inventive and discoverers. Who have minds which can be critical, can verify, and not accept everything they are offered.
>
> **Jean Piaget**

The Digital World Requires a New Set of Skills

News flash: The digital generation has highly advanced skills for functioning in the digital world. Most parents know this from observing their children or playing video or computer games with them, but this is not widely acknowledged by educators. Teachers don't ignore the skill level of their students because they are mean spirited, but because they don't recognize the skills this generation has developed to operate in the digital world.

These new skills don't look like the skills people needed for success in the world of the 20th century. The new skills simply don't show up on teachers' radar. Instead, teachers remain focused on the basic literacy and memorization skills needed for the text-based, nondigital world they experienced growing up and in their time in school and university. And that focus has a devastating effect on students today because they are made to feel academically inadequate and that the things they value are irrelevant.

But who has it right? Today's digital generation does not need the same level of text-based skills to survive and thrive in the digital world. Instead, they have developed advanced visual and cognitive skills needed to handle the bombardment of multimedia, rapid-fire, hyperlinked information that they experience daily in the online digital world. Rather than acknowledging and valuing those skills, teachers zero in on the lack of development in the 20th-century skills that older people value. Instead of building up this generation, we often tear them down and make them feel inferior.

The authors of this book have often heard teachers complain about how students today are not as capable as the students they had in the past. It is true that the digital generation does not possess the skills that previous generations did. But many educators seem to have little understanding why.

Furthermore, many educators have no real understanding of the digital world, so they can't comprehend the significance of what students are capable of doing with the skills they do have. Some educators haven't explored the digital world at all. The authors have actually heard teachers announcing that they have never connected to the Internet as though it was something to boast about. What they don't realize is that they are missing out on something of great significance in the lives of their students. No wonder many of the digital generation are finding it difficult to be in school!

Here is a critical question: Who has the best skill set for succeeding in the increasingly digital world of the 21st century—teachers with 20th-century literacies or the digital generation with 21st-century visual and cognitive skills? It's no contest—the kids do! It is incredibly important for educators to acknowledge that their students are way ahead of them in being able to function in the digital world. If teachers hope to connect with their students, then they must make a concerted effort to catch up to them in experiencing the digital world.

As they enter the digital world, teachers will quickly discover just how impressive the skill set is that the digital generation has developed to navigate, understand, and create in the online digital environment. And the question must be asked: If kids are way ahead of teachers in developing the skills needed to succeed in the digital world of the future, and if teachers are oblivious to the significance of the skills kids have acquired in this digital world, and if teachers are continuing to focus their instruction on the literacies for the 20th century instead of the skills necessary for success in the new digital 21st century, and if a lack of understanding of this new digital world is hampering the ability of teachers to reach their clientele of modern students, then who really has the learning problem?

The answer is obvious: Educators have a huge problem when it comes to acquiring knowledge of this new digital online experience, and they must catch up to their students in developing skills for functioning in the world of the 21st century.

Relevance Is Critical to the Learning Process

There are great benefits for educators if they embrace the digital world their students are experiencing. An understanding of this world will help greatly in making instruction more relevant for learners.

Let's talk for a moment about how this is supported by brain research on effective learning. In his book, *How the Brain Learns*, David Sousa (2005) makes the point that for new learning to stay with a student it must have relevance to the learner. This is an important aspect of learning for teachers to consider when they are designing lessons and learning tasks.

The examples, illustrations, and applications of learning must have significance to the students if we want to maximize the chance that the learning will stick. It can't just be relevant to the teacher, it must be relevant to the students. Ron Zemke (1985) and Richard Saul Wurman (2000) have both used the metaphor of Velcro to underscore the importance of relevance in the learning process. Both these authors stated that having instruction without relevance is like having only one side of a piece of Velcro. This is not what we want in our classrooms. We want to see both come together to create what we call Velcro Learning—when knowledge and relevance combine to make learning stick in the minds of students. It is vital that teachers see the essential role that relevance to the learner plays in effective, long-term learning.

And there's the rub. To create the relevance that is so critical for learning, teachers must know the world of their students. This, of course, was not a problem in the stable world of the 20th century when the world of students was very similar to the world teachers experienced growing up. But today, in the early 21st century, the digital generation is experiencing a world that is radically different from the world most of their teachers knew.

So if we want to have any hope of getting the relevance that is needed for effective long-term learning, then it is of the utmost importance that teachers jump into the digital world with both feet. To help educators get started with this task, we have compiled a list of digital activities that teachers can do in the digital environment.

Dive Into the Digital World

Please note: This is not a list of activities targeted exclusively at teachers. We firmly believe that going through this list of activities should be a required task for anyone involved directly or indirectly in instruction, anyone who creates learning materials, all administrators, politicians making decisions regarding educational budgets and policy, and those responsible for designing learning environments and new school buildings. However, there is a risk in doing this. This digital world is not static. It is a fast-paced, dynamic world where new activities and trends develop overnight. As soon as we put this list on paper, we are dating ourselves. While the activities listed here will definitely give you a good introduction to the digital environment, just remember that there are probably new experiences that are not mentioned here.

The first thing you can do if you want to truly begin to understand the digital generation is to go on the Internet and read the adventures of teenager Jeremy and his long-suffering nondigital parents in the cartoon strip Zits. This will give you a snapshot into their world and what's going on their heads, especially as they have to deal with the nondigital perspective of the older generation.

For those educators who have little or no experience on the Internet, it is important to spend some time exploring the range of what is available. Start with an area of interest and begin searching for information using a search engine like Google. However, while Google is the most popular search engine, it is by no means the only one. Take a look at Yahoo!, Ask, Dogpile, AltaVista, WebCrawler, HotBot, Excite, Lycos, SearchFound, and a whole host of others. It would be tempting to just continue looking for information in an area of interest of the teacher, but the point of this exercise is to gain an understanding of the world of the digital generation. So once you have gained some comfort in searching for information, it's time to shift gears and begin looking for the kind of information kids search for. Start by looking for music (their kind of music—not ABBA or Herman's Hermits). Download some free music files and learn to play them on the computer. Then start looking for the kind of information appropriate for the age group you deal with. This may be entertainment news, sports information, or product specifications.

Now it's time to discover online commerce. Search for an item of interest and purchase it online from a company's web site. Log on to craigslist and eBay. Spend some time exploring the range of goods available for purchase.

It is important that you appreciate the learning potential of the online world. Pick a skill that your students would like to master. It might be learning how to play the guitar or fix a mountain bike. Search the Internet for sites that will help you develop that skill.

To gain an appreciation of the amazing visual skills, lightning-quick reflexes, and rapid-fire decision-making ability of the digital generation, try playing video games with them. To get a feel for their ability to handle the simultaneous bombardment of multiple forms of information, play those games while music is playing and a movie is running in the corner of the screen.

What follows is a list of fun and informative digital activities teachers new to the Internet can do to explore the digital world. Some are personal sites, others are commercial—they're just intended to give you a sense of what's out there.

- Sites for Teachers: www.sitesforteachers.com/. Hundreds of educational sites all ranked by popularity.
- The best on the Web for Teachers: http://teachers.teach-nology.com/. Another web site with hundreds of resources for teachers.
- The Teacher List: www.theteacherlist.ca/.

Summarizing the Main Points

- The digital generation has highly advanced skills for functioning in the digital world, but they lack many skills necessary in previous generations.

- Many educators have no real understanding of the digital world.

- If educators embrace the digital world, it would help greatly in making instruction more relevant for learners.

- Research has shown the importance of relevance in the learning process.

- To create the relevance that is so critical for learning, teachers must know the world of their students.

Some Questions to Consider

- What effect has teachers remaining focused on the basic literacy and memorization skills needed for the text-based, nondigital world had on students today?

- Who has the best skill set for succeeding in the 21st century, and who has the biggest learning problem?

- How is relevance important to the learning process?

- What is Velcro Learning?

- What can teachers do to become familiar with the digital world of students today?

Reading and References

Dryden, G., & Vos, J. (2009). *Unlimited: The new learning revolution and the seven keys to unlock it.* Auckland, New Zealand: The Learning Web.

Gardner, H. (1983). *Frames of mind: Theories of multiple intelligences.* New York: Basic Books.

Johnson, S. (2005). *Everything bad is good for you: How today's popular culture is actually making us smarter.* New York: Riverhead.

Pink, D. (2005). *A whole new mind: Moving from the information age to the conceptual age.* New York: Riverhead.

Prensky, M. (2006). *Don't bother me mom—I'm learning.* St. Paul, MN: Paragon House.

Prensky, M. (2010). *Teaching digital natives: Partnering for real learning.* Thousand Oaks, CA: Corwin.

Sousa, D. (2005). *How the brain learns.* Thousand Oaks, CA: Corwin.

Tapscott, D. (2009). *Grown up digital: How the net generation is changing your world.* New York: McGraw-Hill.

Tapscott, D. (2008). *Wikinomics: How mass collaboration changes everything.* New York: McGraw-Hill.

Trilling, B., & Fadel, C. (2009). *21st century skills: Learning for life in our times.* San Francisco: Jossey-Bass.

Wagner, T. (2008). *The global achievement gap: Why even our best schools don't teach the new survival skills our children need and what we can do about it.* New York: Basic Books.

Willingham, D. (2009). *Why don't students like school? A cognitive scientist answers questions about how the mind works and what it means for the classroom.* San Francisco: John Wiley and Sons.

Wurman, R. S. (2000). *Information anxiety.* New York: Hayden.

Zemke, R. (1985). *Computer literacy needs assessment: A trainer's guide.* New York: Addison Wesley.

Chapter 7

A Shift to Whole-Mind Instruction

> Imagine a school with children that can read and write, but where there are many teachers who cannot, and you have a metaphor of the Information Age in which we live.
>
> **Peter Cochrane**

It is important that we take an honest look at the kind of instruction taking place in schools today. Drop in on a typical classroom anywhere in North America and what will you find? Students still meet with teachers in classrooms that will accommodate 25 to 30 kids just like they have for the last hundred years. You will quickly discover that the basic instructional approach has not changed either. David Thornburg tells the story of a teacher from a hundred years ago being brought back to life and asked to teach in a modern school. Amazingly, this teacher of old would fit in quite well because, while a number of new technologies have been introduced into our schools over that hundred-year period, the underlying approach to instruction has not changed. Teachers still talk and students still listen.

What do they talk about? Teachers spend a great deal of time telling students what they need to know to do well on tests. The focus of the instruction is on getting students to memorize the content in the curriculum. In preparation for unit, end of term, and large standardized tests, teachers give students homework assignments and projects that reinforce the memorization of course material.

Not only do teachers tell students what to learn, they also tell them how to learn it. The most common type of assignment given is the report, a regurgitation of facts, theories, stories, events, and observations made by others and gleaned by the students from their research primarily using the textbook for a course. Most often all learning is completely internal to the classroom and focused on the instructional materials provided by the teacher. Very little from the kids' world is involved at all.

While some research may come from other sources including the Internet, the students do very little analysis of the material they retrieve. In fact, you will find that the vast majority of high school teachers assume that students already know how to do effective research and think critically.

As a result, with the pressure of covering the content outlined in their curriculum guides, most high school teachers do not spend much time instructing students on how to develop the higher-level thinking skills needed for critically assessing the research material they encounter. Elementary school teachers, on the other hand, often believe that students will be given instruction on how to do higher-level critical thinking when they get to high school. Consequently, most of their instruction also focuses on low-level content recall skills.

Teaching to the Test

The primary evaluative tool in schools today remains the test. Students are given short quizzes, end of unit tests, end of term tests, comprehensive end of year exams, and state or provincially mandated standardized exams.

Recently, there has been an emphasis on increased accountability in K–12 education. Well-meaning politicians and educational bureaucrats, motivated by concern with a perceived lack of rigor in public schooling, have latched on to test scores as the prime indicator of how well education is functioning. Consequently, they have required students to take more comprehensive tests much more often to prove they are mastering course content. With so much emphasis being placed on testing in schools today, and in light of the fact that this testing drives so much of what takes place in the classroom, it is critical that we look at exactly what these tests are measuring.

Unfortunately, those in control of education have returned to the schools of their youth for how to make education work. We are seeing the ideas of yesterday being touted as the answer to educating 21st-century students.

What is not widely recognized is that the tests being given to our students are based on 20th-century thinking and primarily measure 20th-century skills. Take a look at the kinds of questions students are asked. You will discover that the majority of questions are in multiple-choice format. These types of questions have been used on tests for a long time because they are the easiest questions to mark, both manually and by machine.

The next thing you will notice is that the majority of questions focus on content recall. The kind of thinking required to answer most of these questions is often at the lowest level in the wide range of types of thinking that people can do. In many questions, students are asked to name, identify, locate, spell, describe, tabulate, list, define, and examine.

It is important to note that these types of questions focus on the low-level thinking skills that were important in the world of industrial life in the 20th century. The vast majority of workers needed to develop these low-level memory skills to accomplish the tasks of their jobs. Whether it was a frontline worker on an assembly line, a loan officer in a bank, a clerk in the records department of an insurance company, or a teacher, being able to memorize the policies and/or procedures for your job was an essential skill. Only the small percentage of managers needed to have the big picture thinking skills to develop new ways of doing things or solve big problems.

In addition to focusing on low-level content recall skills, it is also important to note that paper-based tests have never provided anywhere near a complete picture of student learning. They give no indication of what a student can do. To get a complete picture of learning, a student must be given the opportunity to demonstrate the skills they have acquired.

Students may have constructed a desk; designed and built a web site; written, directed, and edited a documentary film; painted a portrait; participated in a debate; determined the source of pollution in a local creek; created a sculpture of a historical figure; developed a 3-D virtual world that simulates common geological features; taught a concept in mathematics to a fellow student living in another part of the world using interactive online technology; or produced a literary newsletter with editorials expressing opinions on the meaning of *The Lord of the Flies*.

The written tests give educators no idea of these skills. In fact, written tests are so limited in what they measure that they are not used widely for evaluation outside the school system.

Just think of going to the motor vehicle department to get a driver's license. Of course there is a written test to make sure you have memorized the rules of the road, but that is only a small part of qualifying for a license. The major focus is on a practical demonstration of acquired driving skill in a road test in an actual car. This is the same when pilots are certified or electricians become journeymen. And when salespeople or other businesspeople are evaluated in their annual reviews, they are assessed on their performance, not on written tests. Certainly written tests have their place, but it is essential that we realize their limitations in providing a complete picture of student learning.

However, because so much emphasis is placed on the score a student receives on tests, especially the large comprehensive exams, preparation for these evaluations is given a high priority by school administrators. Classroom teachers have naturally responded to the new demands for increased testing, and as a result, many of the supplemental instructional activities and projects that were given to students previously have been abandoned in favor of instruction and assignments that directly prepare students for these tests.

> *... projects that create interest in learning and foster higher-level thinking have been abandoned in order to spend more time on memory exercises trying to boost test scores.*

This is not a pretty picture. Modern digital learners are facing a system that is experiencing a narrowing of focus on the memorization skills of yesterday. To make matters worse, many of the projects that create interest in learning and foster higher-level thinking have been abandoned in order to spend more time on memory exercises trying to boost test scores.

Further, the learning environment is decidedly low-tech, with most teachers still using whiteboards and overhead projectors where they control the flow of information in the classroom. Learning materials are often limited to paper-based black-and-white photocopies—a far cry from the full-color, multimedia, hyperlinked world of instantaneous access to information this generation experiences outside the classroom.

Plus, the skills the digital generation have developed in that world don't fit with what the teachers teach and the tests test. Today's students often comment that they have to "power down" when they go to school. This has created a crisis of engagement in schools today—the digital generation is being bored to tears while teachers try to get them to perform on tests.

But it's worse than just a lack of engagement for students. We are also preparing students for a world that no longer exists. Our whole instructional approach is out of sync with the modern world of the 21st century.

Rethinking the Focus on Memorization

Consider what our focus on memorization communicates to our students about how we see the world of information. The value of committing details to memory comes from the belief that there is a static body of information that a person should know to be considered educated.

This is exactly what E. D. Hirsch espoused in 1988 in his book, *Cultural Literacy*. He identified 15,000 facts he believed students should know to be considered educated. Most of the instruction and testing that takes place in schools today are based on this idea that there is a relatively stable body of information that students must memorize to be successful in life.

The problem is that this is not reflective of the fast-paced, rapidly changing digital world that students experience outside school. Why? Because they have access to a wealth of information through online tools, the scope of which we could not even imagine when we were growing up. And through the experience of navigating this online infoscape, the digital generation has discovered that much of the information in the world is not static. It's changing—daily.

Today's generation has discovered that memorizing is not nearly as important a skill as the skill of knowing how to get the information you require when you need it. Because if you can get information when you need it, then it will be current. For example, students are required to memorize the capitals of the states and provinces. Why? Just in case the student ever needs to know the capital of Wyoming sometime in the next 40 years.

But that kind of information can be easily retrieved from online sources through a computer or cell phone. And by the time they need it, the capital of Wyoming may have moved to a new location. That's what is happening to many of the so-called facts in daily life. They are changing. Pluto is no longer considered to be a planet. Burma is now called Myanmar. New medical procedures cascade into life, such as laser correction for sight problems and a whole host of other ailments. Propulsion systems for cars now include a number of options besides gasoline engines. The environment is being rethought in light of global warming. The list of changes goes on and on. In this environment of dynamic information, being able to access current data is far more important than memorizing specific facts.

This is not to say that there is no need for any memorization. King John still put his seal to the Magna Carta in 1215, Michelangelo still painted the Sistine Chapel in 1512, Einstein still stated his theory of general relativity in 1915, and so on. Of course there will always be a body of information for students to know. But there is an ever-increasing digital source of information available online that is making the very notion of memorization less important than ever before. For example, Google provides the average person access to an already impressive number of information sources that can provide requested information in less than a second—and there is much more coming.

There are several institutions and companies involved in the creation of a universal library—an online digital library of literary works distributed over multiple sites across the Internet. In his May 14, 2006, *New York Times* article titled "Scan That Book," Kevin Kelly outlines the efforts already underway to create this digital library. Google announced in December 2004 it would digitize all of the books in five major research libraries (Stanford University, Harvard University, Oxford University, the University of Michigan, and the New York Public Library). In addition, Google is now partnering with several major publishing companies to digitize vast numbers of out-of-print books and excerpts from books currently in print.

Also in 2004, Raj Reddy, professor at Carnegie Mellon University, began scanning books from his university's library. Called the Million Book Project, Reddy's goal was to have a million books scanned by 2008. Superstar, a company based in Beijing, has scanned every book from 200 libraries in China, which represents half of all the books published in the Chinese language since 1949. There is a rapidly growing digital library of digital books being created.

> *Most of the instruction and testing that takes place in schools today are based on this idea that there is a relatively stable body of information that students must memorize to be successful in life.*

Just think of what these projects will make available when people do searches on the Internet. But this shift to an online digital library is about much more than just access. The magic is in how the information and ideas in one book will be linked to the information in every other book. Imagine being able to jump to each book in a bibliography to see the context of quotes cited in an article, or being able to assemble all of the passages from all digital books on a specific term or concept, or accessing all of the works with an opinion on a particular issue.

But the power of this digital library goes much further than just the linking of information. Kelly (2006) goes on in his article to discuss the creation of personalized compilations of references, quotes, and passages gleaned from the massive library of digitized books. People will create these compilations in an area of research or interest much the same way people create playlists in music programs today.

These literary "idea lists" will then be shared, expanded, annotated, and cross-referenced in the online world. This will greatly alter and extend the pursuit of knowledge, ideas, and opinions. It will also require people to develop whole new skill sets in order to navigate, inquire, analyze, and evaluate in the new digital "ideascape" of interconnected literature. Thus far, we have only been talking about digitizing printed works. What happens when the information in audio recordings and film footage is digitized and cross-referenced to the information in books in the same way?

The generation growing up today is already immersed in the world of access to digital information and they intuitively see the potential of new online search engines such as this new digital library to get them the information they require at a moment's notice. They already have the foundational skills and understanding necessary to grasp the significance of a new digital library of literary works and to put it to work for them in getting the information they will need.

> *It is vital that educators realize that students learn a lot from simply observing how we teach.*

The power of this kind of interconnected, multimedia digital "ideascape" to inform, stimulate, challenge, and engage students will usher in a wonderful new era of learning. It will also force schools to radically shift the focus of their instruction away from the 20th-century standards we currently see in education today. It is critical that everyone involved in education understands that there has already been a significant shift in skill emphasis of the need for memorization in modern life and that shift will continue to occur the further we go into the 21st century. It is vital that educators realize that students learn a lot from simply observing how we teach. Just by getting up and teaching the way instruction has been done traditionally tells students that a teacher is not in sync with the world around them. Modern digital students will increasingly disconnect from school if the shift in focus away from memorization is not reflected in our instructional approach.

Changes in the 21st-Century World of Work

The traditional instructional approach of teachers talking and students listening and memorizing is also not equipping students with the skills they need for the modern world of work. This comes as a real shock to many in education because for so long schools have prepared people for work. During the industrial revolution of the 20th century, the majority of workers needed memory skills to do their jobs. Schools naturally focused on developing those skills in their students. And this approach was very successful for a very long time. But what has not been widely acknowledged in schools is that the world of work has changed significantly from the days of the industrial revolution.

Consider a modern worker participating in a project with a global workgroup. Global companies are now creating worldwide workgroups to expedite projects. Workers pass their work electronically at the end of the day to a branch office located in a time zone where workers are just beginning their day.

Similarly, those new workers pass their work electronically to another branch office located in another time zone where workers are just beginning their working day. This continues nonstop as the work moves electronically around the globe. Projects are worked on 24 hours a day and completed in a fraction of the time it took when work was done in a single office.

This is a completely different working environment than the one that was in the minds of the designers of 20th-century schools and requires significantly different skills than those needed by most 20th-century workers.

The entire environment of the working world has changed due to electronic technology and globalization. Consider the change that has taken place over the last 20 years in the loyalty companies and employees have for each other. It used to be that a person could work for one company for their entire working life. However, today, with contracting out of many jobs, the era of lifelong jobs, union or otherwise, is at an end.

Students in school today face the very real possibility of being entrepreneurs living from one contract to another. This will be the case regardless of the kind of work being done—office work, engineering, laboring, construction, or manufacturing. And the changes continue. The new online digital world is spawning entirely new jobs that didn't even exist a few years ago.

Consider that there are more than a million people who make their living partly or fully on eBay. The fast-paced, continually moving working world of the 21st century will force most young people in school today to move to new careers more than once in their lives. In fact, the Department of Labor in the United States is now projecting that students in school today will have 10 to 14 different careers in their lifetime.

What Educators Must Understand to Prepare the Digital Generation

How do you prepare students for this new digital environment and world of work? What skills do they need to survive? First and foremost, it is important to see that many of the skills schools have traditionally taught are still needed. Shifting to catch up to the modern world does not mean we shouldn't teach the three Rs. It's not an either/or situation. We still need to teach students how to read, write, and perform basic mathematics calculations. But there are three aspects of the new digital world that educators must understand if they are going to effectively adjust their teaching to match the new world of technology and work.

A Shift in Emphasis

First, while we will continue to teach many traditional skills, there will be a shift in emphasis of importance of those skills. This may be an affront to teachers, especially older teachers, who have considered certain skills as vital in preparing students for life.

For example, good handwriting has long been valued by teachers as an important skill for students to acquire because that skill was critical for the paper-based note taking, letter writing, form completion, and report writing that was done in 20th-century industrial life. And while there are still cognitive benefits to learning to write by hand and good reasons to teach this skill to students as they go through school, we must face the fact that the emphasis on handwriting as a critical skill for the world at large has changed significantly over the last 20 years.

The world has shifted to a digital online realm where writing is done almost exclusively using digital software tools (this might not be the case for teachers and other older people, but it certainly is the case for the kids who have grown up in the digital world). This means that handwriting is not nearly as important as a job skill today as it was in the past. It is important that teachers re-evaluate the importance of all the skills they have taught traditionally in light of the realities of the new digital world.

New Basic Skills

The second aspect of the new digital world that educators must understand if they are going to effectively adjust their teaching to match the new world of technology and work is that there are new skills that must be considered as part of the basic literacy skills of any student. These are the essential skills that any person needs in order to function in the world today. These are not necessarily new skills, but they are skills that have become more important in the modern world. Why have these skills received a promotion? The answer is technology.

We have spent a considerable amount of time in this book outlining the changes that have taken place in the world as a result of digital technology. These changes represent a shift of enormous magnitude in the way people experience daily life and how they go about making a living. Changes this immense obviously mean that people will need new skills to operate in the new digital environment. It is important that you recognize that these are not optional skills, but absolutely essential abilities that the average person requires to function adequately in modern society.

As we mentioned previously, these new basic skills do not replace the basic skills needed for 20th-century life. Instead, they supplement and extend those skills. What we are talking about is a superset of skills that includes the literacy skills we have traditionally taught. However, these new skills do represent a significant shift in emphasis in the basic skills that a person needs for success in the modern world.

There are many groups who have compiled long lists of 21st-century skills. We believe that the essential skills fall into six main categories (in addition to the traditional three Rs that continue to be important skills in the modern world). We call these new skill categories 21st-century fluencies.

We prefer to use the term *fluency* rather than *literacy* when describing these skills because it conveys a greater ease with which they can be used. You may be literate in a second language, but you still have to make a conscious effort to think about what you are hearing or reading to decode its meaning. However, when you are fluent in a second language, you have attained such a comfort level with it that its use is unconscious and automatic. Another way to understand what we are getting at is to consider what goes on in your mind when you are using a pen. You don't think about using a pen or moving your hand. Instead, your brain is directly engaged with the message you are trying to receive and record or communicate in your own words. The same thing happens after you have been driving a car for a number of years. You become so comfortable with the skill that your mind is freed to think about other things. All of these examples describe a level of proficiency that transcends mere literacy and reaches the level of fluency.

Solution Fluency

The first of these new essential 21st-century skills is solution fluency. This is about whole-brain thinking—creativity and problem solving applied in real time. Solution fluency is at the core of "just in time" learning, which is essential to function successfully in the culture of the 21st century.

Solution fluency is the ability to think creatively to solve problems in real time by clearly defining the problem, designing an appropriate solution, applying the solution, and then evaluating the process and the outcome.

Information Fluency

The second new essential 21st-century skill is information fluency. There are two subsets of skills under the umbrella of information fluency.

The first subset of skills is the ability to access digital information sources to retrieve desired information. This involves both surfing and searching skills and being able to figure out when to use them to zero in on what you are looking for. People who have information fluency know how to use a wide variety of information sources and searching tools on a variety of digital devices, including computers, cell phones, and handheld devices. Such people also know the appropriateness of various searching tools for retrieving different kinds of information. For example, should you use Google Scholar Search or Facebook when you are looking for biographical information on a current political figure? Accessing skills must include knowing where to retrieve information in various mediums, including text, images, sound, and video.

The second subset of information fluency skills is the ability to effectively assess the information that is retrieved from searches or the content of messages being received. A person can't be considered to have information literacy, let alone information fluency, if all they can do is get information without the ability to critically evaluate the data they find. We are so overwhelmed with the amount of information available to us already that just accessing it is really not helpful.

What is really needed is the ability to find significant information. To be able to assess the significance of information, a person must be able to perceive trends in the digital infoscape. They must be able to discover bias in the information they retrieve. They must be able to assess the accuracy of data they uncover in their searching, including assessing the methodology of how data was gathered, and determine if there are other sources that verify and support the specific information they find.

Collaboration Fluency

The third new essential 21st-century skill is collaboration fluency. In the new digital landscape, collaboration has taken on a whole new meaning. Collaboration fluency is teamworking proficiency that has reached the unconscious ability to work cooperatively with virtual and real partners in an online environment to create original digital products.

Virtual interaction through social networking sites and online gaming domains has become a part of the digital generation's and our daily lives. We are interacting with people all over the world with electronic and wireless communication technology. This has meant the "death of distance," which has tremendous and exciting potential for education.

For example, students learning about civil war could be talking to kids in Kosovo or Iraq or Afghanistan. Students learning a foreign language could work with native speakers of that language who are learning English. Students could work in virtual partnerships on projects with kids from across town or across the world.

Creativity Fluency

Creative fluency is the process by which artistic proficiency adds meaning through design, art, and storytelling. It regards form in addition to function, and the principles of innovative design combined with a quality functioning product.

Creative fluency extends beyond visual creative skills to using the imagination to create stories, a practice which is in demand in many facets of today's economy. It is widely regarded by many successful industries that creative minds come up with creative solutions.

There is tremendous value in the artistic creation of items in order that they may transcend mere functionality.

Media Fluency

There are two components of media fluency: first, the ability to look analytically at any communication media to interpret the real message, determine how the chosen media is being used to shape thinking, and evaluate the efficacy of the message, and second, the ability to create and publish original digital products, matching the media to the intended message by determining the most appropriate and effective media for that message.

We live in a multimedia world, and one of the truly wonderful aspects of it is the ability for average people to communicate their messages with the rest of the world using digital software tools to convey their ideas in a variety of media and then post them for public viewing in the online environment. No longer is publishing for just the few. The digital world has made powerful tools available to virtually everyone, fostering an explosion in communication by ordinary individuals, and in this interactive visual world, our children must be able to create and publish original digital products with which they can communicate just as effectively as they can with text.

The Internet is awash in web sites created by people who have little or no understanding of how to construct digital documents that communicate their messages effectively. It is important for educators to see that excellent writing skills are not enough to be good communicators in a multimedia world. While writing skills provide a great foundation, they are not enough to be effective publishers in the modern world. We believe it is essential that the average person learn the principles of effective design for print, sound, video, web sites, and, soon, 3-D environments.

The idea is to challenge learners to create digital products that reflect their understanding of content, develop technical skills, and provide them with the empowering principles of graphic design.

The Digital Citizen

All the 21st-century fluencies are learned within the context of the digital citizen, using the guiding principles of leadership, ethics, accountability, fiscal responsibility, environmental awareness, global citizenship, and personal responsibility.

The concept of digital citizenship has been the topic of several books, the most comprehensive of which is *Digital Communities, Digital Citizenship: Perspectives for Educators* by Dr. Jason Ohler (2010). There are many aspects to digital citizenship, but we want to take a moment to highlight just one: the need for consistency in personality. It is important that we teach students from an early age that the personality they communicate online is consistent with who they are in person. Many relationships today start online. Face-to-face meetings only happen later. There will be real problems if it is discovered the persona that was portrayed online is not who the individual is in person. This is particularly important as the online world is now moving into three-dimensional virtual worlds like Second Life, where users can create their digital appearance.

Further, it is vital that kids understand the people they encounter online may not be who they portray themselves to be. For example, this can protect them from becoming emotionally attached to an online personality only to discover that person is not really the same way when they want the relationship to progress. But what is more important, kids must understand that there are people who pretend to be other kids, but who are actually adults wanting to exploit innocent young people for money or worse.

Many social networking sites, including Facebook and MySpace, limit access for people under the age of 14. They aggressively remove people for being underage, not to mention having removed many thousands of people for inappropriate or illegal behavior. These sites are serious about trying to make these safe places. But despite all their best intentions, these sites are only as safe as the individual user's ability and skill at making appropriate online judgments that come from a realization that people online may not be what they seem.

While the majority of uses of new online communication tools are positive, anyone using these tools must be aware of the people who are using online tools for financial gain and criminal activity. For young children, this requires the guidance of savvy adults who can help students assess online personalities and environments, because kids are unable to perceive the manipulation that is being done to them.

This is a brief overview of these fluencies. There is much more to say about them, far beyond the scope of this book, and we will discuss them in depth in our upcoming book *Literacy Is Not Enough: 21st Century Fluencies for the Digital Age*. Noticeably absent from this list is any kind of technology fluency. This is because technology has become ubiquitous. It's everywhere, and the digital generation assimilates it as fast as manufacturers can produce it. Give any of them a new digital gadget and they will figure out how it works before you can finish reading the safety precautions in the manual.

Technology isn't the problem anymore, so the 21st-century fluencies are not about technology, but what to do with it. They are process skills and critical thinking skills, and they're indicative of the kind of skills that everyone will need in the digital age.

Higher-Level Thinking Skills for Everyone

The third aspect of the new digital world that educators must understand if they are going to effectively adjust their teaching to match the new world of technology and work is that everyone living and working in the new digital world requires much higher-level thinking skills than were needed for success in the 20th century. We have already introduced this idea when we talked about the need for assessing the information people find in the digital world. Being able to determine the accuracy of information and perceive bias are much more complex cognitive skills than simple rote memorization of details. But the need for higher-level thinking skills goes far beyond being able to assess information.

Before we discuss this further, let's define what we mean when we say higher-level thinking. In 1956, Benjamin Bloom headed a group of educational psychologists who developed a classification of levels of intellectual behavior that were important in learning. This became known as Bloom's Taxonomy of Thinking Skills (Bloom, 1956). It is this classification scheme that gave rise to the idea of higher-level or higher-order thinking skills because the complexity of thought increased as you moved higher up the taxonomy. Bloom and colleagues came up with the following six levels of thought:

6 **Evaluation**	Can the student justify a stand or decision?
5 **Synthesis**	Can the student use new information in a wider context?
4 **Analysis**	Can the student distinguish between the different parts?
3 **Application**	Can the student use the information in a new way?
2 **Comprehension**	Can the student explain ideas or concepts?
1 **Knowledge**	Can the student recall or remember the information?

Many alternatives have been proposed to Bloom's taxonomy, but the value of the general framework has been proven over time. During the 1990s, a new group of cognitive psychologists led by Lorin Anderson, a former student of Bloom's, updated the taxonomy to make it more relevant to 21st-century work (Anderson & Krathwohl, 2001).

We like the updated taxonomy because it reflects the new era of creativity that has been facilitated by the emergence of the online digital world. What we mean when we talk about higher-level thinking is thought that is moving to the higher levels of the taxonomy of thinking skills. This is the kind of thinking that is required for real-world problem solving, information processing, and idea creation.

6 **Creating**	Can the student create a new product or point of view?
5 **Evaluating**	Can the student justify a stand or decision?
4 **Analyzing**	Can the student distinguish between the different parts?
3 **Applying**	Can the student use the information in a new way?
2 **Understanding**	Can the student explain ideas or concepts?
1 **Remembering**	Can the student recall or remember the information?

There is one more point we must address before discussing the need for higher-level thinking skills. That is the need for education to reflect the realities of the working world. The idea of linking public K–12 education to the skills needed for the world of work is a big stretch for many teachers. They argue that it is not their role to prepare students for jobs. From their perspective, getting students ready for the world of work is the role of post-secondary institutions. The problem with this position is that it leaves the majority of students ill equipped for employment because most young people simply don't go to, let alone graduate from, traditional post-secondary programs. The U.S. Bureau of Labor Statistics indicate that only 31 percent of people will have a two- or four-year degree by the age of 30 (U.S. Department of Labor, 2007). This means that 69 percent of the students in K–12 schools will not get their preparation for employment from traditional post-secondary education.

An October 2006 Indiana study (www.incontext.indiana.edu/2006/october/2.asp) appears to indicate that more than 31 percent will have some form of post-secondary education. However, their data includes people who have some college experience but have not graduated. This is misleading because one of the biggest problems in post-secondary education is attrition in or after the first year due to the lack of skills that students have acquired in order to handle college-level work. Ted and Ian have both sat on committees for post-secondary institutions whose sole purpose was to address the attrition problem of students who drop out during or after first year. This Indiana data inflates the percentage of the number by including these students.

While there are a host of new post-secondary training programs like Microsoft Certified Software Engineer courses and the Cisco Certification Program, these new programs require students to develop their information access and processing skills, as well as their ability to solve real-world problems that arise in the workplace. So it is imperative that we look at the world of work and ensure that our instruction reflects the reality students will face upon graduation. Not only will students get the skills they need to survive, our teaching will gain the relevance that is so desperately needed in order to generate the interest required to engage students in learning. With this in mind, let's take a look at the modern working world and the shift that has occurred in the kinds of thinking skills needed for success in 21st-century employment.

The Shift in Employment Today

For well over one hundred years, there have been many jobs that required only the lowest level of thinking skill to be successful. The amazing economic growth of the late industrial revolution was largely due to implementing the ideas of Frederick Winslow Taylor. Taylor came up with the idea of scientific management. The central idea in his thinking was to break down complex tasks into subtasks, each of which could be done by a single worker. They would memorize the procedures for their subtask and do it repeatedly until it became rote. Office work, assembly lines, department stores, schools, and, in fact, all of industrial society were based on Taylor's thinking. The vast majority of workers became specialists, working on their subtasks in much larger processes. Workers received work from other specialists, did their part, and then passed it on to the next person in the chain. Individual workers were not required to think about the big picture. That was left to the small group of managers. Most of the work required only the lowest level of memorization skills for success.

But today, the working environment has changed radically. Just think about the impact the explosion of online information has had on workers. We have already mentioned the higher-level thinking that is required just to assess large amounts of data to determine its significance. Now consider that many companies are ensuring that frontline workers are provided with access to online information relating to their jobs, either through informational resources on local area networks, through access to the Internet, or both. From manufacturing jobs to office work, workers are increasingly expected to find information relevant to their jobs and apply that information to solve problems and/or improve efficiency. Earlier in the chapter, we discussed the new online working environment that has emerged in the 21st century. To be effective in these kinds of jobs, the average worker must be able to function at a much higher level than was needed for success previously. The days of the manager meeting with his or her workers and telling them of his or her decisions are fading fast. Savvy managers now know that it is often the frontline worker who is the best person to include in decision making. In a growing number of businesses, decisions relating to the day-to-day running of the organization are made exclusively by the workers doing the work. Low-level thinking skills won't cut it in this working environment. Instead, an increasing number of workers require thinking skills that are much higher up the taxonomy of cognitive abilities. To make effective decisions about the running of a business, frontline workers must be able to see the big picture of how all the parts of the operation work together to make the whole.

The future for workers who do not possess these higher-level thinking skills is bleak. Consider a world where more and more jobs are being automated and contracted out. In his book, *The World Is Flat*, Thomas Friedman (2005) paints a dismal future for workers who have nothing more than low-level thinking skills. Today, if jobs can be done by machines or robots or they do not require workers to have anything more than low-level thinking skills, the work is being taken away from high-cost North American workers and given to lower-cost contractors, or being completely automated with computers and machines. The career choices for students today have already changed significantly from those children had growing up in the 20th century and will continue to do so in the future. Simply put, if a person does not have the higher-level, big-picture thinking skills we previously discussed, then they are at risk of being replaced by a robot or losing their job to a cheaper contract worker or a worker in another part of the world.

A consequence of this new working environment is that young people today face a future where they will spend part, if not all, of their working life as an entrepreneur moving from one contract to another. In his book, *Free Agent Nation*, Daniel Pink (2002) describes how the phenomenon of free agent entrepreneurs has already become a major segment of the economy. Working as one of these free agents requires a different skill set than working in a traditional job, and it is a skill set with a decidedly higher-level thinking focus. A person needs to be able to do project design, handle problem solving and career planning, and acquire the learning needed for what's next in their working life.

The bottom line here is that a significant shift has taken place in the working world outside the school system. To be properly equipped for employment success in the 21st century, the average person must have much higher-level thinking abilities than ever before. This is a shift that schools must address. When this shift is combined with the pressing need people today have for skills in assessing the significance of the vast amount of information available in the modern world, it is clear that educators must embrace the idea that higher-level thinking skills must now be considered an essential component in the basic skills students are taught to prepare them for the world they will enter upon graduation.

We can't continue to pretend that teaching the way we always have is good enough for our students. So how can we make our teaching effective, relevant, and engaging in the age of the digital generation and the new world of work? How do we shift our instruction to equip students with the higher-level thinking skills needed for success in the modern digital world? The answers to these questions lie in an understanding of how the brain works. We must shift to whole-mind instruction. Let's take a look at how the brain operates to get an understanding of what whole-mind instruction means.

> *… it is clear that educators must embrace the idea that higher-level thinking skills must now be considered an essential component in the basic skills students are taught to prepare them for the world …*

Understanding Whole-Mind Instruction

It has long been known that the brain has two hemispheres, left and right, that perform quite different functions. Using scanning equipment that allows researchers to noninvasively examine live brains in the act of thinking, our understanding of what the left and right hemispheres do has advanced greatly in the last 10 years. Here's what we have discovered. The left hemisphere is sequential. It specializes in recognizing serial events like talking, reading, and writing. It is particularly good at decoding things that march in single file. It handles logic. It deals in the literalness of meaning. The left brain wants to take in images and events and analyze them individually because analysis is what the left brain does best.

The right hemisphere has been more mysterious in its function, but modern technology has begun to reveal its remarkable abilities. The right brain specializes in being simultaneous. In his book, *A Whole New Mind*, Daniel Pink (2005, p. 19) puts it this way:

> *The right side of the brain specializes in seeing many things at once—seeing all the parts of geometric shape and grasping its form or seeing all the elements of a situation and understanding what they mean.*

The brain's right side handles synthesis, emotional expression, context, and putting the big picture together to create meaning. It resolves contradiction to make sense of situations and to determine significance. Pink uses a metaphor to illustrate the different roles the two hemispheres have in determining meaning: "Joe has a heart the size of Texas." In this metaphor, the left brain identifies the contradiction between the size of Joe's heart and the size of Texas. The right brain sees the contradiction in context and determines the real meaning—that Joe is a very kind and loving man.

Here's another example Pink uses to illustrate how the two hemispheres work together. Let's say my wife and I are working on making dinner after a hard day of work. Halfway through the preparation, we discover that I forgot to buy a key ingredient in the recipe. My wife grabs the car keys and hisses, "I'm going to the store." My left brain determines the literalness of her words and actions—she has the keys and she is going to Safeway in the car. But my right brain sees those otherwise neutral words in context and determines the bigger meaning—she's upset! The point here is that to determine the real meaning of what is happening in situations requires much more than just the capabilities of the left brain. Higher-level thinking always involves the right hemisphere. In fact, it always involves both. Higher-level thinking is a whole-mind activity.

Schools have traditionally focused on left-brain thinking, and with good reason. Left-brain thinking was the basis of the incredible success of the industrial revolution. As we mentioned, Taylor's idea of breaking down tasks into subtasks is at the heart of scientific management. And it is a left-brain focus. So too is the logical sequential reasoning required to do things in the industrial revolution environment that was spawned by Taylor's approach. From assembly line workers to office workers to teachers, this was the approach you needed for success. And so schools focused on left-brain thinking in instruction. There was an emphasis placed on developing specific skills needed for discrete tasks, such as memorizing details and proficiency in basic reading, writing, and arithmetic skills. In this world, only managers needed big-picture thinking skills.

But along comes the information age of the 21st century, where many of the tasks of the industrial revolution are being automated or outsourced. What we are left with besides "McJobs" are jobs where people have to see the meaning and significance in huge amounts of data available in the online world. They need to be able to see the big picture in the information they access and to use that knowledge to solve problems and accomplish tasks. This environment requires that all workers have the higher-level big-picture thinking skills that only managers needed in the industrial revolution.

Our Conclusion

And there's the rub—schools have not recognized the changes that have occurred in the world around them and have continued to teach as if it were 1980. Yes, schools are now equipped with computers and networks, but the basic instructional approach has not changed significantly. And the skills students develop in their education are not a fit with the world outside school. Politicians, educational bureaucrats, and teachers continue to emphasize lower-level memorization skills in preparation for standardized tests. This cannot continue. It is imperative that schools shift gears to catch up with the new online world of instantaneous access to more information than we could have imagined only a few years ago. The world today is crying out for high-level thinkers. Thinkers who use both sides of their brains to be truly effective at applying all of human reasoning to 21st-century tasks.

Thus, it is critical that we come up with teaching strategies that help students develop these big-picture thinking skills. The key is to teach to the whole mind. But what does whole-mind instruction look like? What changes must we make to shift our instructional approach to mirror the shifts that have already taken place in the world outside school? In his book, *Teaching for Tomorrow* (2005), Ted McCain identifies six changes teachers must make to shift their instruction to reflect the realities in the modern world and equip students with the big-picture thinking skills they need for success in that world. Let's look at how some of the changes he proposes address the need for higher-level thinking skills for the 21st century.

One of the key changes Ted identifies is that teachers must make a fundamental shift—problems first, teaching second. This represents a complete inversion of current instructional practice. Just think about the order of business in most classrooms. The teacher spends some time at the beginning of the class talking about the subject matter in the lesson to be covered. Some questions may be asked of students to check that they understand what has been presented. Then students are given an assignment to complete that reinforces the content in the instruction. This might be an in-class task using the textbook or photocopied material or it may involve completing questions written on an overhead display or whiteboard. The assignment might be a larger task that students continue at home as homework outside class time. This is the traditional approach to instruction—teaching takes place first, tasks or problems follow.

> *... teachers must make a fundamental shift—problems first, teaching second.*

The difficulty with this model of instruction is that it is the opposite of the way learning happens most of the time in the world outside school. For most people in most situations, problems or tasks come first and learning comes second. If the task to be accomplished or the problem to be solved requires skills or knowledge we don't have, it creates the motivation for new learning. This applies to personal problems as well as work-related tasks. We discover that a family member has a drug abuse problem and we are motivated to search the Internet for rehabilitation programs. We decide to replace the bathroom door in our home, so we head down to the building supply store to learn how to hang a new door. We see a tree dying in our front yard, so we phone the local garden center to find out what is wrong and what can be done about it. Our boss asks us to reconfigure the sales computers to handle a recent change in the sales tax, so we phone the government department responsible for taxation to learn about the changes. A client asks us to create an interactive web site with an animated introduction, so we buy a book that explains how to use the "Flash" program. We discover that the promotion we want requires applicants to have knowledge of accounting, so we enroll in a night school basic accounting class. Almost without exception in life outside school, problems or tasks come first and learning comes second. If we hope to adequately prepare our students for success in life after school, then we must shift our instruction to reflect the reality of how tasks and problems are encountered in the world outside school.

To make this happen, teachers must make a fundamental shift to an instructional approach that begins with the problem that students must solve. It is critical that the problem be presented before teaching the students how to find the solution. Ted outlines such an approach that uses role-play to present tasks to students. He suggests that teachers pretend they are clients or bosses who need something from the people who work at a company or organization (the students). This is a wonderful way to bring the real world into the classroom. This approach has two significant benefits. First, students immediately recognize the relevance of the learning when it is presented in this manner. Second, giving students the task before giving them any instruction forces students to use higher-level thinking skills to determine what is needed by the client or boss. It also forces them to think about what they will need to learn in order to do the work being asked of them. This opens the door to shift the ownership of the responsibility for learning from the teacher to the student.

Ted sets a goal in his classes of only teaching what students ask him to teach, and nothing more. This significantly changes the role of the student in the classroom. They become responsible for determining the instruction they need to accomplish the task. This in turn opens the door for students to seek out the kind of teaching that suits them best. For example, if digital students learn better from interactive information on the Internet than from traditional classroom instruction, then they could pursue online learning. On the other hand, if they decide they need instruction from their teacher, then they could ask for teaching in the classroom.

This approach significantly changes the role for teachers as well. To ensure that students are led into asking questions that come from the curriculum for the course, the teacher must become an expert in crafting problems. This will require teachers to step outside the box of their current thinking about what lessons look like and how they are presented. They will have to work on converting the content in their curriculum guides into problems for students to solve. Creating these tasks that engage students in the content of a curriculum and that challenge them to do higher-level thinking requires great skill.

Teachers and administrators are so concerned about getting higher test scores, they are afraid to let their students loose to work without constant direct supervision.

Another change Ted identifies is that teachers must progressively withdraw from helping students. This is not what happens in most schools today. Teachers and administrators are so concerned about getting higher test scores, they are afraid to let their students loose to work without constant direct supervision. Teachers tell the students everything they need to know and how to go about learning it. This approach is used right up until students graduate from high school. While this approach can have some success in getting students to perform on exams, the problem is that the experience makes the students dependent on their teachers. They do not develop the skills necessary to do learning and solve problems on their own. Ted suggests that teachers adopt a strategy of deliberately pulling back from assisting students over the course of a year. If possible, this strategy should be employed over the entire course of a student's time in school.

By withdrawing from helping students, teachers force their students to learn and apply the mental skills necessary to function independently. This can only be done if students are equipped with a process to follow when they encounter new problems or tasks. Ted outlines a structured problem-solving process called the 4Ds that students can use for solving any problem:

- Define the problem.
- Design the solution.
- Do the work.
- Debrief the effectiveness of the work that was done.

It is beyond the scope of this book to delve any deeper into the 4Ds problem-solving process. For any teacher wishing to explore this problem-solving approach to instruction, we recommend that you read *Teaching For Tomorrow* (McCain, 2005).

There is one additional benefit to adopting the strategy of progressive withdrawal. As the teacher stops telling students how to do the learning required to accomplish the tasks in the classroom, the students gain more freedom to pursue 21st-century learning styles that are foreign to the teacher.

Summarizing the Main Points

- Tests being given to our students today are based on 20th-century thinking and primarily measure 20th-century skills.

- Kids today have discovered that memorizing is not nearly as important a skill as the skill of knowing how to get the information you require when you need it.

- Working environments in the 21st century require significantly different skills than those needed by most 20th-century workers.

- There are three aspects of the new digital world that educators must understand if they are going to effectively adjust their teaching to match the new world of technology and work: a shift in emphasis, new basic skills, and higher-level thinking skills.

- The digital generation needs to be able to see the big picture in the information they access and to use that knowledge to solve problems and accomplish tasks.

 Some Questions to Consider

- How do you prepare students for the new digital environment and world of work? What skills do they need to survive?

- What new skills must be considered as part of the basic literacy skills of any student?

- How have 21st-century working environments changed?

- What is whole-mind instruction, and why is it important in education today?

- Why must teachers withdraw from helping students?

Reading and References

Anderson, L., & Krathwohl, D. (2001). *A taxonomy for learning, teaching and assessing—A revision of Bloom's taxonomy of educational objectives:* New York: Longman.

Bloom, B. (1956). *Taxonomy of educational objectives.* Boston: Allyn & Bacon.

Dryden, G., & Vos, J. (2009). *Unlimited: The new learning revolution and the seven keys to unlock it.* Auckland, New Zealand: The Learning Web.

Friedman, T. (2005). *The world is flat: A brief history of the twenty-first century.* New York: Farrar, Straus and Giroux.

Friedman, T. (2008). *Hot, flat, and crowded—Why we need a green revolution and how it can renew America.* New York: Farrar, Straus and Giroux.

Gardner, H. (1983). *Frames of mind: Theories of multiple intelligences.* New York: Basic Books.

Hirsch, E. D. (1988). *Cultural literacy: What every American needs to know.* New York: Vintage Books.

How do education, age and gender relate? (2006) InContext, Vol. 7, No. 10. Indiana Business Research Center at Indiana University's Kelley School of Business.

Jukes, I. , McCain, T., & Crockett L. (2010). *Literacy is not enough: 21st century fluencies for the digital age.* Kelowna, BC: 21st Century Fluency Project.

Kelly, K., (2006) *Scan this book!* http://www.nytimes.com/2006/05/14/magazine/ 14publishing.html. New York Times, May 14, 2006.

McCain, T. (2005). *Teaching for tomorrow: Teaching content and problem-solving skills.* Thousand Oaks, CA: Corwin.

Ohler, J. (2010). *Digital communities, digital citizenship: Perspectives for educators.* Thousand Oaks, CA: Corwin.

Pink, D. (2002). *Free agent nation: The future of working for yourself.* Chicago: Business Plus.

Pink, D. (2005). *A whole new mind: Moving from the information age to the conceptual age.* New York: Riverhead.

Sousa, D. (2005). *How the brain learns.* Thousand Oaks, CA: Corwin.

Tapscott, D. (2008). *Wikinomics: How mass collaboration changes everything.* New York: McGraw-Hill.

Tapscott, D. (2009). *Grown up digital: How the net generation is changing your world.* New York: McGraw-Hill.

Trilling, B., & Fadel, C. (2009). *21st century skills: Learning for life in our times.* San Francisco: Jossey-Bass.

US Census Bureau report on educational attainment in the United States, 2003. (2004). p. 2–4. U.S. Department of Commerce Economics and Statistics Administration.

Wurman, R. S. (2002). *Information anxiety.* New York: Hayden.

Chapter 8

Teachers Must Move Off the Stage

> We don't receive wisdom; we must discover it for ourselves after a journey that no one else can take for us.
>
> **Marcel Proust**

As we have mentioned, there has been increased pressure recently on schools to improve test scores. Legislation in the United States and other countries has raised the stakes for getting students to perform well on written tests. Funding, and even the jobs of teachers and administrators, is contingent on how well students do on tests. This heightened expectation of success on tests has made teachers feel it absolutely necessary to tell their students the things they need to remember to score well on the exams. It's a no-brainer for teachers, really. As we mentioned, teachers talking and students listening is the way instruction has taken place for a long time. Talking was the prime method for teaching throughout the 20th century. Teachers with a university education had acquired a thorough knowledge of the subjects they taught and were well equipped to impart this knowledge to their students. So when the pressure is put on teachers to get their students to perform on tests, they employ the teaching technique they have seen the most and is most natural to them. The problem is that the 20th-century model of instruction with the teacher expert standing at the front of the room and talking to students won't work with the digital generation.

The Traditional Model of Instruction Is Not Working

There are two main reasons why the "teacher as expert talking to students" model of instruction is not working today. First, it's getting much harder to be an expert. This was becoming increasingly difficult during the latter part of the 20th century, but it has become impossible during the early 21st century. Why? Because the amount of information in the world has grown exponentially.

According to research from the University of California in Berkeley, the world produced five billion gigabytes of digital information in 2003. That's like a stack of books that reaches one-third of the way from Earth to the sun. But that's nothing!

According to *As the Economy Contracts, The Digital Universe Expands* (Gantz & Reinsel, 2009), a white paper paper from IDC, our digital universe totaled 500 exabytes, or 500 billion gigabytes of data. Since 2007, our annual digital output has exceeded our capacity to store it. If we assembled 500 exabytes into books, it would be a stack that reached to Pluto and back 10 times! At the current growth rate, that stack of books is growing 20 times faster than the fastest rocket ever made: the Atlas V that powered the NASA Pluto New Horizons spacecraft that left Patrick Air Force Base on January 19, 2006. It took that spacecraft 13 months to reach Pluto. It would take our growing stack of books 3 weeks.

The impact of this explosion of new information is most notable in technical fields. Well over 90 percent of the scientists who have ever lived are alive today. As a result, the amount of new technical information being produced each year is staggering. But what is not as widely recognized is the amount of new information that is being generated related to literature, history, geography, politics, art, and music. The sheer volume of new information being generated in the modern world in any field is staggering, making it impossible to be an expert in the traditional meaning of the word. In many cases, digital generation students with access to up-to-date sources of information are more expert than the teacher, especially if all the teacher is focusing on is the memorization of details.

Second, talking at students doesn't work anymore. (In fact, it never did.) Think back to when you were in school. When the door of the classroom closed and a lesson began, what did the majority of your teachers do? If your experience was like most people, they talked and they expected students to sit and listen. This type of teaching likely began when you were in fourth or fifth grade. You really ran into it in junior high school. For those of you who went on to college or university, this lecture style of instruction was the norm. Teachers telling students what they need to know pretty much sums up what happens in most classrooms in most schools even today. So if that many teachers use the same approach, it must be a good way to teach, right?

Wrong. Research has consistently shown that having students sit and listen to a teacher is one of the least effective ways to teach. Figure 8-1 illustrates the conclusions of research done by Edgar Dale on the retention rates of students when they experience various methods of instruction. Dale examined a continuum of teaching methods ranging from students passively receiving new information to students actively engaged with new information.

The Learning Cone

Dale first developed the learning cone of experience in the 1960s. It was often misrepresented by those who added numbers to the cone. Hundreds, if not thousands, of misrepresentations have been created. But the validity of its message has been reaffirmed by subsequent research since then and adapted again and again. For example, the learning pyramid that was developed at the National Training Lab in Bethel, Maine, in 2003 verified the validity of Dale's original work. In 1998 in his book, *The Quality School*, William Glasser added approximate percentages of the amount of information that a person retains two weeks after receiving various forms of instruction to Dale's work. While there may be debate over the exact percentages, what Dale's Learning Cone reveals is consistent with what any teacher knows: Learning increases when students become more active in the learning process.

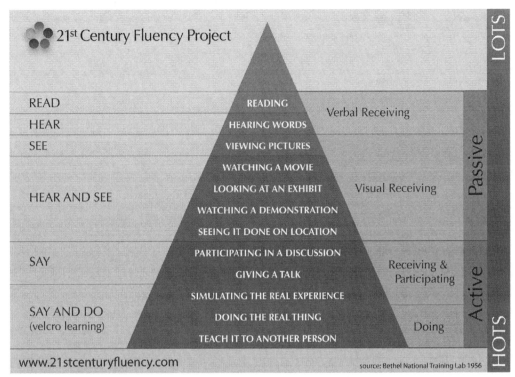

Figure 8.1 *Source: Bethel National Training Lab, 1956, designed by Lee Crockett*

It is clear that the least effective teaching occurs when students are expected to passively receive instruction. The learning cone shows us that talking at kids is one of the worst approaches a teacher can use. What is surprising is that this has been known for some time. Yet most teachers, especially teachers in junior high school, senior high school, and in post-secondary institutions, continue to teach this way. Why? The reason is that so many teachers have used this approach for such a long time, it is the only method of instruction they have ever experienced. Getting teachers to even consider another way of instructing is met with blank stares, quiet resistance, incredulity, or outright hostility. There is a deeply entrenched comfort level with teaching as talking.

But not only do we know that teaching as talking is ineffective, it's going to get a lot worse. The digital generation has grown up with highly interactive, hyperlinked, multimedia, online digital experiences where they control the path through the information and the pace that they move. Can you imagine the difficulties they are going to have just sitting still in a classroom where the teacher talks, let alone retain any of the information being spoken? And when the teacher stops talking, what are the students usually expected to do? They are expected to read from textbooks or from black-and-white photocopies or printed worksheets. Reading was shown as the least effective teaching method in the cone of learning long before the digital generation existed. How do you think the digital generation will do with this approach after experiencing full-color, full-motion, audiovisual animations, videos, and 3-D worlds?

A Disconnect in Learning Styles

As we have outlined, there is a huge disconnect happening in schools today between the learning styles of modern students and the traditional teaching-as-talking approach to instruction. To make matters even more tenuous for schools, there is a narrowing in the definition of what teaching is supposed to look like occurring in the public school system in the United States and many other countries around the world. Politicians trying to improve the education system have latched onto the idea that what is needed is more accountability. Unfortunately, the indicator they have chosen as a measure for success is performance on standardized tests. These tests are a 20th-century evaluative tool that measure 20th-century skills with an inordinate emphasis on rote memorization. Since so much is riding on how well students do on these tests, teachers have been forced to narrow their focus in the classroom to ensure students are prepared to come up with the right answer. Activities and projects that employed teaching strategies higher on the cone of learning have been abandoned in favor of exercises that focus on low-level information recall. These teaching strategies largely use talking and reading to communicate with students, approaches that we have just seen in the cone of learning that are the least effective ways to teach. Unfortunately, with the best of intentions, political leaders are compounding the problems school face in dealing with the digital generation.

It is vitally important that teachers embrace approaches to instruction that emphasize active engagement of students with the information in a subject if they hope to be effective with modern students. So how do teachers move off the stage? How can we teach differently when virtually all the instruction we have ever seen modeled is teachers talking to students? In *Teaching for Tomorrow* (McCain, 2005), one of the major changes teachers must make that Ted identifies is "resisting the temptation to tell." Since this is the most common instructional approach that is modeled throughout the entire school system, there is a strong tendency for teachers to teach the way they have been taught and begin telling students what they need to know. This is especially the case if the students will be responsible for lots of content on an upcoming test. However, this is an ill-advised approach to take with today's digital generation. We have already seen from the learning cone that talking at students has never been very effective. It is even less so with the students who have been raised in the digital world because they are not accustomed to passive listening. They are used to highly interactive digital experiences. They crave active participation in whatever they are doing. Having them sit in rows while the teacher talks is not going to be very effective. Ted points out that telling takes the excitement of discovery out of learning. It is far better for students to discover the content in a course than to be told the content in a course because discovery creates the interest that gets kids engaged in learning.

So if you're not going to tell students what they need to know, how are they going to learn it? The answer is that teachers must shift their instruction from talking to a project-based learning approach. This approach is likely new to many teachers, and it will take some work to master it. But the rewards in terms of student engagement will be worth the effort. Let's look at what this approach entails and how it could be implemented in your classroom. In addition to *Teaching for Tomorrow*, one of the best resources for this kind of learning is the

Project Based Learning Handbook from the Buck Institute for Education (2003). The authors define project-based learning as:

> ... *a systematic teaching method that engages students in learning knowledge and skills through an extended inquiry process structured around complex, authentic questions and carefully designed products and tasks. This definition encompasses a spectrum ranging from brief projects of one or two weeks based on a single subject in one classroom to yearlong, interdisciplinary projects that involve community participation and adults outside the school.* (p. 4)

A key aspect to this approach to learning is that the project is used to engage students in the central concepts and principles of a course. The authors of *the Project Based Learning Handbook* highlight the importance of this shift in instruction.

> *Often, projects have been used as fun or change-of-pace events completed after students have been pushed through homework assignments, lectures, and tests. In Project Based Learning, students are pulled through the curriculum by a Driving Question or authentic problem that creates a need to know the material.* (Buck Institute for Education, 2003, p. 5)

They stress the essential role the project plays in getting students engaged in the content of a discipline:

> *The project work is central rather than peripheral to the curriculum.* (Buck Institute for Education, 2003, p. 4)

With the project as the prime vehicle for delivering the curriculum through a discovery approach, students can be asked to develop real-world, higher-level thinking skills that exercise both sides of their brains. The *Project Based Learning Handbook* underscores this point:

> *More important, evidence shows that Project Based Learning enhances the quality of learning and leads to higher-level cognitive development through students' engagement with complex, novel problems.* (Buck Institute for Education, 2003, p. 6)

The authors outline the key attributes of outstanding projects. Following is a list of some of the features of effective projects:

> *Require the use of essential tools and skills, including technology, for learning, self-management, and project management.*
>
> *Specify products that solve problems, explain dilemmas, or present information generated through investigation, research, or reasoning.*
>
> *Include multiple products that permit frequent feedback and consistent opportunities for students to learn from experience.*
>
> *Use performance-based assessments that communicate high expectations, present rigorous challenges, and require a range of skills and knowledge.*
>
> *Encourage collaboration in some form, either through small groups, student-led presentations, or whole-class evaluations of project results.* (Buck Institute for Education, 2003, p. 4)

In *Teaching for Tomorrow* (McCain, 2005), Ted extends the idea of using project-based learning with the role-play strategy for presenting problems and tasks to students that we referenced previously. Essentially, the teacher takes on a role of a person in the world outside school, like the owner of a local business, or the editor of a magazine, or a government biologist. Students are asked to take on real-world roles as well. They become web site designers who have been contacted by the local business owner who wants a web site, or writers for the magazine who have been given a new article to write by their editor, or field biologists who have been asked to investigate a chemical spill in a river. Ted then goes on to describe a problem-solving process called the 4Ds (Define the problem, Design the solution, Do the work, and Debrief what you have done). By teaching this process to students, they become equipped with the tools they need to solve the problem that has been presented to them in the role-play.

The beauty of this instructional approach is that it is both effective at engaging students in learning as well as helping them to remember what they have learned. Engagement is generated from the discovery aspect of this kind of learning. Instead of being told, students use the 4Ds to become detectives searching for the answers they need to accomplish the task they have been given. Helping students remember what they have learned comes from the context provided by the real-world task. Context creates a frame of reference for remembering new information. For example, if a teacher simply told students that the annual rainfall for their area was 22 inches per year, the chances are very good that students will forget that piece of information very quickly, if they remember it at all. However, if the students are given the task of determining which plants will be best suited for the landscaping for a new government building, then knowing how much precipitation is received in the area becomes a critical piece of data for choosing the plants for the landscaping. As we have already discussed, research has demonstrated that the application of learning creates longer lasting memories. Students move right to the top of the learning cone because they become active doers in searching for the information they need, then analyzing and applying the information to accomplish the task they have been given.

Students develop the whole-mind thinking skills we described previously. By asking students to define a task, design its solution, do the work, and debrief what they have done, they must do big-picture, right-brain thinking to see how all the parts fit together to create the whole project. This is in addition to the left-brain thinking involved in the logic, computation, and sequencing required to create the various parts of the solution to the problem.

This is good news for teachers struggling to prepare students for standardized tests. Project-based learning can help students remember. This was documented in a Bertelsman Foundation study done in Michigan in 1998. One hundred eighth-grade students were taught social studies using a traditional approach. Students sat in rows while they were lectured on the course content. These students were given traditional content-focused tests. Another group of 100 students were taught the same curriculum using nontraditional, project-based methods. Evaluation was a combination of student self-evaluation and joint student—teacher assessment. At the end of the year, the students in both groups were given the same traditional standardized test. Their scores were identical. However, one year later the students were given the same traditional standardized test. The results were dramatically different. The students who had been taught using traditional methods scored less than 15 percent on the test and indicated that they saw social studies as the memorization of isolated facts. The group that had been taught using a project-based approach scored more than 70 percent on the test and indicated that they saw social studies as the study of complex relationships in the world.

This instructional approach allows the teacher to move off the stage. They no longer have to be the center of attention, or the one who is responsible for disseminating all the content for a course. The students now take on the onus for finding the information they need. The teacher becomes a facilitator who helps guide the students to the answers they seek. This is a much more effective strategy for teachers to employ when trying to engage modern digital students in the learning required to cover the curriculum of a course in school. It shifts the focus from the teacher to the student and, in the process, greatly increases the interest generated by class projects. It is far more engaging than the relentless focus on drill-type activities requiring only lower-level thinking skills in order to regurgitate often-meaningless facts so that students will perform well on some standardized test. By moving off the stage and inviting students to become involved in projects that ask meaningful questions that relate to the larger world outside school, teachers not only provide the context needed for better memory recall, they require students to develop higher-level, right-brain thinking skills that will serve them well as they make the transition into the rest of their lives.

Summarizing the Main Points

- The 20th-century model of instruction with the teacher expert standing at the front of the room and talking to students won't work with the digital generation.

- The digital generation has grown up with highly interactive, hyperlinked, multimedia, online digital experiences where they control the path through the information and the pace that they move.

- There is a huge disconnect happening in schools today between the learning styles of modern students and the traditional teaching-as-talking approach to instruction.

- It is far better for students to discover the content in a course than to be told the content in a course because discovery creates the interest that gets students engaged in learning.

- The 4Ds problem-solving process equips students with the tools they need to solve the problem that has been presented to them by the teacher.

Some Questions to Consider

- Why is the traditional model of instruction not working?

- What does Dale's Learning Cone tell us about retention rates of students when they experience various methods of instruction?

- How do teachers move off the stage? How can we teach differently when virtually all the instruction we have ever seen modeled is teachers talking to students?

- What is the 4Ds problem-solving process?

- How does the 4Ds problem-solving process incorporate right-brain and left-brain thinking?

Reading and References

Buck Institute for Education. (2003). *Project based learning handbook: A guide to standards-focused project-based learning for middle and high school teachers*. (2nd ed.). Novato, CA.

Dryden, G., & Vos, J. (2009). *Unlimited: The new learning revolution and the seven keys to unlock it*. Auckland, New Zealand: The Learning Web.

Gantz, J., & Reinsel, D. (2009, May). *As the economy contracts, the digital universe expands*. Framingham, MA: IDC.

Gardner, H. (1983). *Frames of mind: Theories of multiple intelligences*. New York: Basic Books.

Glasser, W. (1998). *The quality school*. New York: Harper.

McCain, T. (2005). *Teaching for tomorrow: Teaching content and problem-solving skills*. Thousand Oaks, CA: Corwin.

Pink, D. (2005). *A whole new mind: Moving from the information age to the conceptual age*. New York: Riverhead.

Prensky, M. (2010). *Teaching digital natives: Partnering for real learning*. Thousand Oaks, CA: Corwin.

Reeves, T. (1998). *The impact of media and technology on schools*. Bertelsmann Foundation. itech1.coe.uga.edu/~treeves/edit6900/BertelsmannReeves98.pdf

Richardson, W. (2008). *Blogs, wikis, podcasts, and other powerful web tools for classrooms*. Thousand Oaks, CA: Corwin.

Trilling, B., & Fadel, C. (2009). *21st century skills: Learning for life in our times*. San Francisco: Jossey-Bass.

Chapter 9

Teachers Must Let Students Access Information Natively

> We can no longer afford to educate today's students for tomorrow's world with yesterday's schools.
>
> **John Chapin**

What exactly does the title of this chapter mean? What is accessing information natively? It means that young people who have grown up in the digital world will use new digital tools while employing strategies that are foreign to older people who grew up in a different nondigital world. Why is this important? Because nondigital older teachers are frustrating their students with their lack of understanding of the power of these new digital tools and the centrality they have in the way the digital generation lives their lives today. It is critical that teachers grasp these two key aspects of the digital world because the digital generation knows them implicitly just by functioning in the digital world. Let's discuss them for the benefit of our nondigital readers.

Key Aspects of the Digital World

First, there is great power in new digital tools to communicate and accomplish tasks in ways that are completely outside the experience of older people. What can be done with digital tools is astonishing in terms of its speed, its global reach, its access to unheard of amounts of information, and its ability to connect with huge groups of people. This alone can be hard for older people to understand, but what is even more bewildering is that the effective use of these tools requires thinking processes that are completely different than anything older people have ever experienced. Not only are older people amazed at what younger people can do with these new tools, they are left wondering how they did it. Following are a few stories illustrating the power of these tools and the new thinking that is being used to make them effective.

In his book, *Here Comes Everybody*, Clay Shirky (2008) tells the story of a man named Evan who used the incredible new power of the online digital world to get his friend's lost cell phone returned. It is a story that illustrates the power of the digital world to influence daily life. Evan's friend, Ivanna, left her cell phone, a $300 multifunction SideKick with keyboard and camera, in a taxicab and thought it was gone forever. Ivanna purchased a new phone and had the information from the old phone (which had been saved on the phone company's servers) transferred to her new phone. When that happened, Ivanna discovered photos taken by the person who now had her phone. These photos were of Sasha, the girl using the phone, and her boyfriend, Gordo. Ivanna asked Evan to help her get in touch with Sasha. Because Sasha had emailed the photos from the phone to her friends, Evan had her email address. He emailed Sasha and asked her to return the phone. Sasha not only refused to return it, she made a violent racial threat toward Ivanna and Evan.

Now if this had happened a few years ago, it would have been the end of the story. Even though they knew who had the phone, they had no real leverage to get it back. But this wasn't a few years ago, and the new online world provided Evan with some powerful publishing and communication tools that previously weren't available to the average person. Evan decided to create a web site called "StolenSideKick" to tell his friends what had happened and documented each new step in the saga. His friends were outraged by the story and began forwarding the information around the Internet. One of those friends found a MySpace page containing the photos of Sasha and Gordo and passed this information back to Evan. Evan updated his web site with the new material. That evening (remember this is still the first day the information was posted on the Internet), a man named Luis, who said he was Sasha's brother and a member of the military police, emailed Evan. He told Evan to stop harassing his sister and hinted that there might be a violent response if he didn't. Also that evening, the story was posted on Digg, a collaborative news web site where users suggest stories and vote on the newsworthiness of the articles that are posted. The site gets millions of visits each day. The response to the story was overwhelming. That evening Evan started receiving 10 emails a minute from people around the world offering support and assistance in getting the cell phone returned.

Buoyed by this response, Evan began documenting what was unfolding in his communications with Sasha and any other related developments. Evan wrote 40 updates to the story in 10 days, and he had lots to say. Now people who had never met Evan or Ivanna became involved. Someone had discovered Sasha's address and had driven by and taken photos and passed this information back to Evan. A NYPD officer contacted Evan and told him how to file a complaint against Sasha so the police would take notice. However, when he went to the local NYPD precinct, he was told that since the phone was lost, not stolen, the police would do nothing about it. After that information was posted on Evan's web site, he was contacted by another NYPD officer who told him how to file the complaint so the department would treat the phone as stolen. City government officials contacted Evan offering to help deal with the intransigence of the police department. Members of Luis's military police unit contacted Evan wanting to investigate the alleged threat of one of their MPs against a civilian. Then CNN and *The New York Times* picked up the story. The public airing of the NYPD's refusal to treat this case as a theft generated so many complaints that the department had to reverse its stand. The end result was that about two weeks after the story was posted on Evan's web site, Sasha was arrested and the cell phone was returned.

Shirky comments on the importance of this story. He highlights rapid growth in the power that the digital world has to influence daily life. He says:

It isn't a worldwide media event every time someone loses a phone. The unusualness of this story, though, throws into high relief the difference between past and present. It's unlikely that Evan could have achieved what he did even five years ago, and inconceivable that he could have achieved it ten years ago, because neither the tools he used nor the social structures he relied on were in place ten years ago. (Shirky, 2008, p. 11)

And that's what we have been saying throughout this book. The world has changed significantly in the last 10 to 15 years—so significantly that for those who live in the new online digital world, there are entirely new ways for people to accomplish things. These new approaches to getting things done are a mystery to those who are not participants in the new digital culture.

Here is another story that illustrates the significance of this shift in how things get done and how baffling this new world is for those who grew up before it sprang into existence. Shirky's (2008) book also documents a new phenomenon called flash mobs that demonstrates the power of networked devices like computers and cell phones to organize people to gather for social or political purposes. One particular set of flash mobs Shirky describes is especially illuminating. He tells how groups of young people are gathering to protest the repressive actions of the government in Belarus. Using email, blogs, cell phone calls, and texting, messages were sent out to protesters to gather and do a specific activity at a specific place and time. For example, protesters met in Oktyabrskaya Square in Minsk to show their displeasure over the government's harsh treatment of protesters who gathered in that square during the presidential election in 2006. Only this time all the protesters did was meet and eat ice cream together. The police were alerted to the large group of young people meeting in the square, but they were at a loss for how to respond. They knew something organized was going on, but didn't know how it was planned or what they were doing exactly. Eventually, they arrested some of the protesters. These arrests were recorded in photographs and videos taken with cell phones. These images were posted on blogs and shared from person to person. The repressive actions of the state were clear for the world to see when images of police arresting young people for eating ice cream were shared around the globe on the Internet.

> *The world has changed significantly in the last 10 to 15 years—so significantly that for those who live in the new online digital world, there are entirely new ways for people to accomplish things.*

Similar flash mobs were organized to do things such as meet in the square and read the newspaper the day the government announced it was shutting down the Nasha Niva newspaper for printing articles that were uncomplimentary toward the state. Another flash mob was created to walk around the square and simply smile at each other. Each time the actions of the police were recorded and shared with the world. The power of these protests comes from the fact that the mobs are spontaneous so they cannot respond quickly enough to prevent the group from forming, and even if the police are alerted, they have no idea who is going to show up so they cannot take any pre-emptive action against individuals. Plus, since the activities are so mundane and nonthreatening, the police are put in an incredibly bad light if they react. The effectiveness of these flash mob protests relies completely on new ways for young people to behave using the new online digital tools that have emerged over the last 10 to 15 years.

In addition to providing innovative new ways for groups to form, these new communication tools have quite literally created the global village that was first envisioned by Marshall McLuhan. Unlike their parents and teachers, the community of friends and acquaintances for students today includes people from around the world. This was brought to light recently when a teenager's plans to commit suicide in England were stopped when his Facebook friend in the United States contacted police in England. Also, a Canadian teenager was responsible for averting a violent attack on a school in Britain when he alerted authorities to threatening messages he had read online.

But these new digital tools are not being used just for social purposes. Very real work in the business world can be done using these new tools. In the last 20 years, digital tools have greatly increased the productivity of the average worker. Software programs for word processing, databases, spreadsheets, accounting, desktop publishing, engineering design, and x-ray analysis, just to name a few, have empowered workers with skills in using these tools to do considerably more work than those who do not. But there is a new dimension to the use of these software tools that has radically changed the way the world of work operates. It is the use of these tools in combination with the new digital communication tools over the Internet. People around the world are now connected like never before, and as a result, New Delhi is now a suburb of New York and Lahore is now a suburb of Los Angeles.

Thomas Friedman (2005), in his book *The World Is Flat*, talks about the remarkable use of online digital tools by people living overseas to do real work in North America. His book documents a surprising amount of work being done in a wide range of sectors of the economy, from customer service call centers to legal services to accounting work to medical consultations to engineering work. There is even a firm in India offering personal business assistants to people in North America. These assistants will schedule meetings with co-workers, contact suppliers, deal with customer service issues, set up daily schedules for managers, set up conference calls, manage expense accounts, and a whole host of other duties that were previously done by personal secretaries and administrative assistants. It used to be that people competed for jobs with those who lived in their community. Now people are competing on a global stage and this global competition is forcing everyone to look at the value they add to a product or service in order to get a job or stay in business.

> *People around the world are now connected like never before ... New Delhi is now a suburb of New York and Lahore is now a suburb of Los Angeles.*

In a conversation with Jaithirth Rao, an accountant in Mumbai, India, whose company does tax returns and provides accounting services for North American businesses, Friedman summarizes the incredible shift that has begun as a result of digital productivity and communication tools operating on the Internet:

> *What you're telling me, I said to Rao, is that no matter what your profession—doctor, lawyer, architect, accountant—if you are an American, you better be good at the touchy-feely service stuff, because anything that can be digitized can be outsourced to either the smartest or the cheapest producer, or both.*
> (Friedman, 2005, p. 14)

Creating Change in the World

Due to the astonishing capabilities of these new online tools, it is easy to focus on their power as the major factor in creating change in the world. That would be a mistake. The real major factor that has created such amazing change in the world is the mindset that guides their use. Here is a story that illustrates this point and highlights a serious issue facing education. We were recently involved in helping a school district in Wyoming plan for a new high school. One of the consultations we did involved getting feedback from students on what was both good and bad about their current schools, as well as ideas they had for addressing those issues in the new school. The school district had just implemented a program for giving all high school students a laptop computer that had wireless access to the Internet and district staff was keenly interested in seeing the kinds of interesting things the students were now doing in the classes with these devices. The responses from the students were not very positive. Their frustration was captured by a ninth-grade girl who complained that she didn't like carrying around a heavy computer in her backpack when none of her teachers let her use it very much.

The stories we have told in this chapter clearly show that laptops computers connected to the Internet have great power to communicate and accomplish real tasks, and we haven't even mentioned their ability to edit photos and videos, publish traditional and online publications, and create multimedia presentations. So if these computers had so much power, why didn't the teachers of this ninth-grade girl (and a whole lot of other teachers as well) let her use this powerful tool to do her schoolwork? Because the use of this tool is not in the mindset of people who did not grow up using it. Shirky makes an astute observation about the change created by technology:

> *Revolution does not happen when society adopts new technology; it happens when society adopts new behavior.* (Shirky, 2008, p. 160)

The reason the teachers didn't let this student use her laptop was that although the technology was adopted by the school district, the teachers had not adopted new behaviors that would utilize the power of the technology in learning. And until that happens, nothing of significance will be done with that laptop or any other new technology including cell phones, iPods, iPhones, xBoxes, Wiis, and so on.

However, the students like the ninth-grade girl we just mentioned have grown up using these digital tools ever since they were cognizant of the world. The younger generation has adopted entirely new behaviors that make digital tools central to the way they lead their lives. This is a key point. The digital generation cannot function without digital tools. And that leads us to the second reason we must let students access information natively. New digital tools are the prime method for students to connect with their culture.

Immediate Action Is a Hallmark of the Digital Generation

We remember our own children asking for cell phones as they entered their teenage years. We marveled at how quickly they adopted these devices into their daily lives. Then we were shocked at how attached to them they became, this being demonstrated any time they left their phone behind or their batteries lost their charge. We had cell phones and they were a very useful tool, but our concern over not having our phone never even closely reached the level of concern our children felt when they didn't have their phones. We were annoyed; they were desperate. But watching how they used cell phones to connect with their friends revealed the reasons for their desperation. They didn't just use the phones to talk with their friends; they used them to make social events happen. They and their friends had adopted entirely new behaviors for arranging social events like parties, going bowling, playing road hockey, shooting hoops, and so on. Furthermore, they were now a part of a culture that continually monitored what was happening in the lives of their immediate friends, their acquaintances, and a much larger group of loosely connected young people. The way they did things was completely foreign to us. They did not plan events the way we did when we were young. Instead, they used the power of immediate communication to arrange things on the fly. In the course of a single evening they would go to a party with one group of friends, then go bowling with another, and then watch a video and play computer games at one of their friend's houses with yet another group of people. They would manage to do more things in one evening than we did in a month when we were growing up. Ted calls this spontaneous ad hocism, the ability to use digital tools to form new groups of friends to make a social activity happen immediately. This notion of immediate action that occurs spontaneously is a hallmark of the digital generation. And older people must understand this if we hope to get a handle on the digital culture of younger people. If we don't, we will miss connecting with students today and we will always be on the outside looking in on them while we wonder how their culture works. This bewilderment over digital culture is illustrated by a story from our colleague, Lee Crockett.

Lee owned a restaurant in Penticton, a small community in central British Columbia. Every day on his way to or from work, Lee would encounter a street musician named Adam. Over the course of a few months, Lee interacted with Adam and eventually befriended him. Adam was a talented musician who just couldn't function well in a real job environment. Lee found that out firsthand because Adam, frustrated with trying to make a living as a musician, kept asking Lee to hire him. Finally, Lee gave in and hired him on at the restaurant. Unfortunately, after three days Adam said he just couldn't do it. He went back to busking on the street, playing to passersby for change. However, they remained friends, and wanting to support his music, Lee worked out an arrangement where Adam could do odd jobs, on his own rather random schedule, of course.

One day when Adam was in the restaurant, he asked Lee if he could start doing an "Open Mic" night for local musicians because there was no place for people to play. As an artist and musician himself, Lee welcomed the opportunity to support local developing talent and they decided that Open Mic would take place on Thursday nights. Lee said they would start in a month because it would take time to get posters done, take out an ad in the paper, and book some radio spots in order to market the event. Adam looked at Lee as if he was crazy and told him that they would start on the following Thursday and he'd have the place full. Adam asked Lee to just trust him and to go ahead with preparations. Lee ordered the food, booked extra staff, and rented a sound system. On the Monday before the first Open Mic night, Lee started to worry about what he had done. He had now committed to spend more than $2,000 and he was concerned about Adam's ability to market the event. Lee asked Adam how he had promoted Open Mic night. Was he handing out flyers? Adam said, "Nope," and just kept playing his guitar and drinking coffee. On Tuesday, Lee asked Adam again if he was promoting the event, and Adam said, "It's too soon." At this point, Lee realized he had made a big mistake in letting Adam do the promotion and he resolved himself to losing most of the $2,000. Lee let go of the idea of the event being a success.

Then on Thursday night, more than 100 young people crammed into Lee's restaurant. He was astounded. The night was a huge success, but as far as Lee could tell, Adam had not done anything to promote it. Lee could not fathom how Adam had gotten those young people to show up. He was on the outside of this new culture looking in with bewilderment. When asked how he got the people there, Adam said that on Wednesday night he sent a message about the Open Mic night to all his friends on Facebook and asked them to pass the word on to their friends. Then on Thursday, he sent out a reminder because he was worried that Wednesday was a little too early to arrange anything with his friends. There was no other marketing done—none of the posters or flyers or radio spots or TV announcements or newspaper ads Lee was accustomed to using to reach people of the older generation. Lee didn't spend a penny on promotion, yet he had just hosted one of the most successful Open Mic nights the city had ever seen. He was stunned.

Many parents and teachers are having an experience very similar to Lee's. They watch in bewilderment as they observe the way students live their lives. The older people don't understand the attachment young people have to their digital tools or the power these tools have for communication and accessing information. What we must understand is that the use of these digital tools from an early age has altered the brains of the younger generation. In his book, *The Brain That Changes Itself*, Norman Doidge (2007) talks about the culturally modified brain (p. 287). This is a use of certain parts of the brain in specific ways that all members of a specific group or culture share in common as they do the same tasks in the same way according to the norms adopted by their group. This is what has happened in the younger generation. They have developed a digital culture brain that enables them to use the power of new technology to communicate and accomplish tasks in ways that are not only foreign to older people, they are difficult, or even unattainable, for older to people to duplicate. And because these new behaviors are so new and so foreign, the way teachers and administrators use digital tools is too often nonsensical to younger people. The older generation barely uses digital tools in the work they have students do in school or they ban the use of them completely. In so doing they communicate to the digital generation that they have an irrelevant, nondigital life experience that does not connect with what kids experience every day. This is a clash of cultures, and it is a huge issue facing education today. There is a critical need for parents, teachers, and administrators to develop a new mindset that acknowledges and embraces the digital culture of young people. There's one more part of the story of Lee and Adam that is relevant to our discussion of the differences between the cultures of older and younger people. It is Lee's response to what happened.

> *. . . we must acknowledge the centrality of digital tools in the lives of our students and in life in general in the 21st century.*

Lee did not passively remain in his confusion over how Adam made the Open Mic night a success. Instead, Lee became proactive. Having a background in marketing, Lee quickly realized he had no knowledge about this new way this generation was operating, and he knew he was missing the boat on something big. He rolled up his sleeves to re-educate himself about how they functioned in this new networked environment. He wanted to know what marketing looks like in the digital culture and how it could be done effectively. Lee realized that a big part of his clientele had changed (in addition to the restaurant, he also owned a graphic design and marketing firm) and he had better do some quick learning if he hoped to be effective at reaching these people in the future. That effort has paid big dividends because Lee has been able to develop new strategies for reaching the digital generation that have kept him successful at what he does.

Teachers Must Develop a New Mindset

So what about teachers? Hasn't a big part of our clientele changed? In fact, hasn't all of our clientele changed? Have we rolled up our sleeves to re-educate ourselves about how students function in this new online digital world? We don't want to be looking in on this new digital culture with bewilderment. We don't want to be continually wondering why the teaching strategies that used to work with the older generation aren't working with the digital generation today, while we accuse modern students of being less capable than their parents or blaming them for our inability to connect with this new digital culture and to esteem their clever uses of digital tools to do things we never dreamed possible. So if we hope to teach the digital generation, then we must connect with their culture. We must develop a new mindset that includes new digital tools as central to the way life is lived. And we must acknowledge that even though we gain some understanding into how they use these tools to communicate and get things done, to some extent we will always be outsiders looking in. We must allow them to access information in a way that is native to their new life experience and learn from them because they will use strategies that we just don't get.

It is critical that we understand that the digital generation has adopted new behaviors that utilize new technology in new and innovative ways that are completely foreign to older people. It is important that those of us who did not grow up with digital tools realize that we can't expect to just observe these behaviors and then immediately think we can do what they do. That is why we must let our students access information natively. We must let them use the new behaviors they have developed to harness the power of new technological tools to do extraordinary things in ways that we simply don't understand.

Therefore, teachers must adopt a new mindset for the use of digital tools in school. There are three key aspects to this new mindset. First, we must acknowledge the centrality of digital tools in the lives of our students and in life in general in the 21st-century, both as a means to connect to modern digital culture and to do real work in the online "flat" world. If digital tools are central to 21st-century life, then they must be central to what we ask students to do in school. It's not enough just to use digital tools as add-ons to our existing 20th-century approach to instruction, which is the way many teachers use digital tools today. Since teachers have been told to use technology, they add a nonessential use of digital tools to an existing project. Worse, students are only allowed to use technology when they get their traditional assignments completed. Then they are allowed to blast aliens or surf the Internet for a few minutes. The digital generation sees through these superfluous and gratuitous uses of technology a mile away and they do more harm than good because they only reinforce students' feelings that the schoolwork their teachers give them is out of touch with the realities of the modern world. This 20th-century approach only increases the students' feelings of the irrelevance of school.

It is vital that teachers make the use of digital tools central to projects that students do. We must explore the use of digital tools that can enhance learning. It can start with a tool as simple as a word processor. Word processors are virtually ubiquitous and they are very powerful for teaching the logical thought behind the writing process. When used effectively, a word processor is a fantastic tool that facilitates multiple drafts of writing, makes it easy for peer editing of rough drafts, provides numerous proofing tools for correcting and refining written work, and empowers students to publish their work in many different formats including print, web sites, and movies. There are many more software programs and online tools that can greatly enhance the teaching of project planning and the brainstorming of ideas, locating research information, and data analysis, as well as tools for presenting the final product of project work in various multimedia formats. When these tools are central to the work students are asked to do in school, students immediately see the relevance to their lives. Furthermore, students doing projects that use digital tools in meaningful ways develop skills that will serve them well in 21st-century life.

Acknowledging the centrality of digital tools to the culture of the younger generation leads naturally to the second aspect of the new mindset teachers must adopt to be successful in teaching the digital generation. We must explore new methods of instruction that use new digital tools as an integral component in teaching traditional and 21st-century skills. This is obvious. If these tools are inextricably linked to modern digital culture, then using them for learning is a given. However, the years teachers have spent growing up and teaching in a nondigital or slightly digital world make it difficult for many educators to see instruction from a digital perspective. Embracing digital tools as central to learning will take real effort. While we are not saying that teachers have to abandon everything they have ever done, they certainly must let go of the idea that just because an instructional approach worked when they went through school, it will work today. In the fast-moving world of the 21st century, we cannot even hold on to the idea that just because an instructional approach worked 10 years ago, it will work today. Current teaching methods must be re-evaluated in light of the rapid emergence of digital culture. Teachers should be asking these kinds of questions for every lesson they prepare: Can digital tools be used to make the learning relevant for students who have grown up immersed in the use of digital tools? Can digital tools enhance the learning so that it is more effective than a nondigital approach?

Teachers must also let go of the idea that teaching the digital generation will be comfortable. It probably won't be. The world has shifted so significantly in the last 15 years that most students can't relate to many of the experiences that teachers accept as normal. They are not normal today, and if teachers are going to connect with their new clientele of students immersed in digital culture, then they must let go of much of what they think the life of a young person is like. And that will be disorienting. It will be uncomfortable. In fact, a certain level of discomfort in the teacher is likely a good indication that they are on the right track with what they are doing with their students. Now, of course, everything that is digital is not better than traditional teaching methods, but even if it is comparable, then the gains in terms of relevance to digital culture make it worth embracing.

So how can digital tools be used to enhance our instruction? Just what kinds of things can we do with the digital generation? It is beyond the scope of this book to provide an exhaustive coverage of all the possible uses of digital tools for learning. Our goal here is to help teachers develop a new mindset that is open to the potential these tools have for creating relevance and enhancing instruction. However, it may be useful to look at a few examples of how digital tools can assist with learning to help teachers see how adopting this new mindset can help them greatly with instructing the digital generation.

Let's consider the use of a digital tool that is now virtually ubiquitous in the modern world—the word processor. This tool is a boon to anyone with some writing to do. It is so powerful for drafting, editing, proofing, and publishing written work that it is now the standard tool throughout the publishing industry. No one wanting a job in publishing today could even get in the door, let alone survive a single day on the job, without word processing skills. Yet the word processor is still not a standard tool in English classes in the K–12 school system where students are taught to write. The reason is not that the tool is not applicable to writing—the soft copy editing features of the word processor and its graphical components for creating layouts support every step of the writing process from planning to drafting to revising to proofing to publishing. The reason is also not that schools don't have enough computers to put word processors in English classrooms. Schools and school districts across North America have reassigned, recycled, or just plain thrown out many computers over the last 20 years that have all had word processing capabilities and could have been used in writing classrooms. These machines may not have been the latest generation of computer, but they were very capable of enhancing the teaching of the writing process. The major reason they have not been used for teaching writing is that the use of the word processor for teaching writing is not in the mindset of English teachers. And by not using this digital tool, English teachers have missed a great opportunity to enhance the teaching of the writing process, to equip students with 21st-century writing skills that will serve them well in the future, and to connect with the digital culture of their students.

Another digital tool that is making its way into more and more classrooms is the web browser that allows teachers and students to explore the World Wide Web on the Internet. However, again the mindset of the teachers is, in many cases, limiting the effectiveness of the use of this tool in the classroom. Now certainly the use of the browser is a step in the right direction toward connecting with the digital generation, but the way it is used is frustrating the younger generation. Teachers want to access the Internet to get words. They are often locked into a 20th-century mindset of what research and learning information look like. They have students search for articles and text-based information that can be used in the production of traditional reports and essays. Many teachers think that they have joined the 21st century because they get their students to include photos, illustrations, and graphs in their project work. We are not saying that there is no place for this kind of project, but we are saying that the mindset behind a focus on these kinds of projects is greatly limiting the power that the Internet has to create 21st-century communications, and this mindset is greatly frustrating the digital generation. Anyone who has had students use computers connected to the Internet should stop for a moment and think where the students want to go to get information about the world or to learn some new skill. They immediately head off to YouTube to watch videos of world events, or see what their favorite sports or entertainment figure is doing, or to listen to their favorite music, or to see how to play the guitar, or how to fix their mountain bike, and so on. For the digital generation, information is multimedia. And for the rest of the world outside school, that is the way information is going as well. If our mandate is to prepare students for the world they are going to graduate into, shouldn't students be taught the skills needed to retrieve, process, and publish this kind of multimedia information in school? And wouldn't using this kind of information help greatly in connecting with them? After all, digital multimedia is a big part of the native language of the digital generation.

> *Teachers want to access the Internet to get words. They are often locked into a 20th-century mindset of what research and learning information look like.*

A digital tool that almost all students have access to that has potential to enhance learning is the cell phone. Yes, the cell phone. In his book, *Don't Bother Me Mom—I'm Learning*, Marc Prensky (2006) says this about learning with cell phones:

> *What can children possibly learn from a cell phone? Simply put the answer is "anything, if educators design it right." Among the most successful, time-tested, and effective ways of learning are listening, observing, imitating, questioning, reflecting, trying, estimating, predicting, what-if-ing, and practicing. All of these can be done through our cell phones.* (Prensky, 2006, p. 130)

So if these devices have the potential to support learning, why aren't they being used in schools? Almost every kid has a cell phone these days, so the use of them in school would certainly connect with their world. Why are schools banning them? The answer is that the older teachers and administrators have a 20th-century mindset for what learning looks like, and cell phones don't register in that paradigm as a serious tool for learning. But here are a few of the things cell phones can be used for in school: They can allow students to send text message contributions to class discussions or for quick polling of student opinion on an issue, both while students are in the class and when they are away; cell phones can be used for Internet access anywhere, anytime, both in the class and when students are exploring outside the classroom; the GPS system in newer cell phones can be used to teach arithmetic and geometry; news services will send out messages to cell phones with updates on world events that can be used in current event projects; and students can use the cameras in their phones to take photos and videos of businesses, industrial operations, manufacturing plants, historical buildings, and interviews with local politicians or anyone else with information relevant to a school project. Using these devices in school could help students with learning while they also develop valuable 21st-century skills.

Computer games are digital tools that have great appeal to the digital generation, and they also have great potential for learning. Anyone who has children today knows that kids like to play digital games. They know that games are a big part of digital culture. But what many people don't recognize is that games are now a big part of 21st-century life. Prensky (2006) cites several examples of how games are figuring prominently in the modern working world. One surprising use of games is happening at New York City's Beth Israel Hospital, where Dr. James Rosser is requiring his surgeons to prepare for surgery by playing games. Dr. Rosser is the head of laparoscopic surgery, and he has observed that surgeons who have played video games before performing surgery have 40 percent fewer errors than those who do not. The Untied States military is also using games extensively for a wide range of instruction, including teaching tank commanders how to function in the dynamic ground battlefield and teaching pilots how to deal with fast-paced, ever-changing modern air combat. Businesspeople are now noticing that those people who have played games are better at decision making than nongamers, and an increasing number of businesses are giving preference to game players when hiring. In his book, *Everything Bad Is Good for You*, Steven Johnson (2005) notes that playing computer games engages kids in complex three-dimensional worlds that challenge their minds on many levels. He notes that, by all the standards we use to measure cognitive development, game playing has substantial cognitive benefits, including memory, visual memory, decision making, and problem solving. Gaming also develops skills in the use of computer interfaces, the ability to interact over computer networks, and the ability to have spatial awareness in virtual worlds. These are all skills that people will need to function in the rapidly emerging networked digital world that is transforming business and leisure activities. Prensky talks about how the digital generation intuitively understands that game playing develops life skills for a digital world:

> *The true secret of why they spend so much time on their games is that they're learning things they need for their 21st-century lives.* (Prensky, 2006, p. 5)

So why don't digital games figure prominently in the learning students do at school? The answer is that games do not figure prominently in the mindset teachers and administrators have for what learning looks like. But like the word processor, the Internet browser, the cell phone, and a whole host of other digital tools, digital games are inextricably linked to modern digital culture. They are a vital part of the native language that the digital generation speaks today. And if we want to connect with these kids, we must let them speak their digital language in school.

The third key aspect of the new mindset we must adopt to be successful with the digital generation is that teachers must recognize and value the expertise they have in harnessing the power of digital tools to communicate and to do real work. As we have outlined in this chapter, the digital experiences kids have outside the classroom are in many ways better preparing them for life in the 21st century than much of what they learn in school. The skills they develop using digital tools equip them with skills that will serve them well later in life. And because they have developed many of these skills while they were very young, they are much better at performing digital tasks than we could ever be. It is important that we not only recognize this, but we must also esteem the level of 21st-century skills they have acquired. That means we must allow students to use these skills as they do their schoolwork. Our role in the classroom is to craft problems and tasks that will lead our students into the material in the curriculum of the courses we have to teach. Using the strategies outlined in *Teaching for Tomorrow* and the *Project Based Learning Handbook*, teachers can design learning tasks that challenge students to engage with new information as they think their way through the various steps in the project. We must then ensure that students have access to all the tools and resources they will need to perform the task they have been given. Then, in many cases, our job is to get out of their way as they access information in ways that are completely foreign to us. This will be a great challenge because many of their 21st-century literacy skills do not look at all like the traditional literacy skills we grew up with. However, we must value these skills because they enable our students to do real work and further develop expertise that will serve them well in a digital world.

Summarizing the Main Points

- Nondigital older teachers are frustrating their students with their lack of understanding of the power of new digital tools and the centrality they have in the way the digital generation lives their lives today.

- The major factor that has created such amazing change in the world is the mindset that guides the use of digital online tools.

- The use of digital tools from an early age has altered the brains of the younger generation.

- We must allow kids to access information in way that is native to their new life experience and learn from them because they will use strategies that we just don't get.

- Teachers must adopt a new mindset for the use of digital tools in school.

Some Questions to Consider

- What are the key elements of the digital world?

- How can digital tools be used to enhance instruction?

- What are three key aspects of the new mindset teachers must adopt?

- Why are digital devices not being used in schools?

- How is what kids today are learning outside of school better preparing them for life than what they learn in school?

Reading and References

Buck Institute for Education. (2003). *Project based learning handbook: A guide to standards-focused project-based learning for middle and high school teachers* (2nd ed.). Novato, CA.

Doidge, N. (2007). *The brain that changes itself: Stories of personal triumph from the frontiers of brain science.* New York: Penguin.

Friedman, T. (2005). *The world is flat: A brief history of the twenty-first century.* New York: Farrar, Straus and Giroux.

Hutchison, D. (2007). *Playing to learn: Video games in the classroom.* Westport, CT: Teacher Ideas Press.

Johnson, S. (2005). *Everything bad is good for you: How today's popular culture is actually making us smarter.* New York: Riverhead.

Kolb, L. (2008). *Toys to tools: Connecting student cell phones to education.* Eugene, OR: ISTE.

McCain, T. (2005). *Teaching for tomorrow: Teaching content and problem-solving skills.* Thousand Oaks, CA: Corwin.

Pink, D. (2005). *A whole new mind: Moving from the information age to the conceptual age.* New York: Riverhead.

Prensky, M. (2006). *Don't bother me mom—I'm learning.* St. Paul, MN: Paragon House.

Prensky, M. (2010). *Teaching digital natives: Partnering for real learning.* Thousand Oaks, CA: Corwin.

Richardson, W. (2008). *Blogs, wikis, podcasts, and other powerful web tools for classrooms.* Thousand Oaks, CA: Corwin.

Shirky, C. (2008). *Here comes everybody: The power of organizing with organizations.* New York: Penguin Press.

Trilling, B., & Fadel, C. (2009). *21st century skills: Learning for life in our times.* San Francisco: Jossey-Bass.

Chapter 10

Teachers Must Let Students Collaborate

> Collaboration, publication, peer review, and exchange of precompetitive information are now becoming keys to success in the knowledge-based economy.
>
> **Donald Tapscott**

A few months ago, Ted was sitting in the Vancouver airport waiting for a flight when he noticed the young woman next to him working feverishly on her laptop computer. She had at least five windows open on her desktop and kept flipping back and forth between them, copying and pasting information from one to the other. While she worked, she was continually talking on her cell phone. In addition, she had an online chat session running on one side of her screen. When she finished working and put her computer away, Ted leaned over and told her that he could not help but notice the frenzied work she was doing on her computer. She told him that she had been working on a report that was due in her Denver office within the hour.

Ted was impressed and was about to return to his reading when the young woman added that she had been working with five other people on the project. Since she was sitting alone in the airport, Ted asked her how she did that. She responded by saying that she was on her cell phone with a worker in Vancouver, she was online chatting with two different workers in Seattle and San Francisco, and she was emailing back and forth with another worker in Denver, while receiving files from all of them as they worked simultaneously on a collaborative work web site called Basecamp. Once all the project participants had finished doing their parts, this young woman had finished the formatting and submitted the report to her boss electronically. She was pleased that she had finished quite early—she had submitted the report a full 17 minutes before the deadline!

Collaboration Is Key to Productivity in the Digital World

For people who grew up in a non-networked world, this kind of working environment is almost incomprehensible. It is a work anywhere, online workplace where collaboration is key to productivity. The idea of this level of collaboration can be a challenge for many older people to grasp. They were not prepared for this kind of world when they grew up. The collaboration that the young woman in the Vancouver airport was involved in is not the same as the collaboration that happened when most of us were in school. What happened then was that we were sometimes asked to work in pairs, and on even more rare occasions we were allowed to work in small groups. For most of the time, it was a highly competitive environment where your grades were yours and yours alone. You guarded your ideas and did not let others see your work. You worked alone. It mirrored the competitive industrial revolution business environment. In that environment, people often worked in isolation on their one specific part of a much larger process, whether it was in manufacturing, insurance, banking, retailing, or, in fact, the vast majority of businesses. But today, more and more people are working together on joint projects, both personally and professionally. And they are using digital tools to do it. If teachers are going to connect not only with the world of their students, but also equip those students with relevant skills for their future lives, then it is critical that teachers grasp the extent that collaboration has spread across the modern world.

The digital generations accept the idea of working with people online as completely normal. By the time they have reached school, many will have already played games with online friends. They have probably never seen these online friends, and they could live anywhere in the world. By the time students have reached fifth or sixth grade, they definitely will have interacted with online personalities, most likely to play games. Many of these games reward group collaboration. By the time they have reached their teens, kids will be very comfortable interacting with and working with people online for personal and recreational activities. They will also have used other networked devices to communicate instantly with their peers. Cell phones and handheld computers are essential communication tools for the digital culture. We have already discussed how young people are using digital tools to communicate and create a spontaneous culture. These tools are facilitating a whole new way for them to form groups for recreational activities. Collaboration is the way people are connecting, whether it is through their cell phones or over the Internet to share personal information, to play games, to share photos and videos, or to create shared repositories of useful information.

Mass Collaboration Creates Real Value

In his book, *Wikinomics*, Donald Tapscott (2008) discussed the collaboration phenomenon that is sweeping across modern society. He comments on the essential role collaboration has played in the development of online tools that the digital generation now uses daily to enhance their personal and recreational lives:

> *. . . how ordinary people and firms are linking up in imaginative ways to drive innovation and success. A number of these stories revolve around the explosive growth of phenomena such as MySpace, InnoCentive, flickr, Second Life, YouTube, and the Human Genome Project. The organizations are harnessing mass collaboration to create real value for participants and have enjoyed phenomenal successes as a result.* (Tapscott, 2008, p. 2)

In this quote, Tapscott also mentions another area of life that has been greatly affected by mass collaboration. It is the accumulation of knowledge and research. He talks about the amazing collaborative work done on the Human Genome Project. Collaboration has become an indispensable method for applying the power of collective thought to create intellectual work of great value to mankind. Wikipedia is another great example of how mass collaboration can create an intellectual work of real value and great utility for all members of society. Researchers are now collaborating with one another because it is no longer possible for any one person to keep up with all the developments in any particular field. The only way to get the latest knowledge and techniques applied to a particular problem is to open up the problem for many people to see.

But this idea of collaboration goes much further than just personal, recreational, and research use. Mass collaboration is sweeping across the business world, radically altering the way work gets done as it spreads to small and large firms alike. In fact, Tapscott's (2008) book *Wikinomics* is completely devoted to documenting how mass collaboration is changing the way business gets done. Even large, long-established businesses are benefiting from the use of digital tools for collaborating:

> *Companies such as Boeing, BMW, and Procter & Gamble have been around for the better part of a century. And yet these organizations and their leaders have seized on collaboration and self-organization as powerful levers to cut costs, innovate faster, co-create with customers and partners, and generally do whatever it takes to usher their organizations into the 21st century business environment.* (Tapscott, 2008, p. 2)

Tapscott begins *Wikinomics* with the story of Goldcorp, a Toronto-based gold mining company. In March 2000, Goldcorp was in dire straits. Faced with dwindling ore in the ground at their Red Lake mine, combined with rising costs for extraction, Goldcorp was not in a good position to handle falling gold prices. They needed to find more gold, or the future of the business looked very bleak. Company engineers estimated it would take several years to do the exploration work needed to find new ore deposits. The company didn't have that long. Their new CEO, Rob McEwen, decided to implement a radical new approach to exploration—one that would stand the mining industry on its head. He made all of the company's geologic information on their mining property available for the world to see, and he challenged anyone to come up with ideas for where to look for gold, offering a prize of $575,000. Now for anyone with a 20th-century business mindset, this is contrary to everything known about how business works. A company's information is sacred and vigorously guarded. Work is done in-house and only by those who have proven trustworthy. To put these guarded secrets on the Internet for anyone to see, and to invite anyone to work for you without checking out their background, is sheer lunacy. And yet, that's exactly what McEwen did. The business minds of the day mused at Goldcorp's folly and debated how long they could stay in business.

What happened? Within a very short time, Goldcorp received 110 suggestions from all over the world for where to drill for gold, and more than 50 percent of these locations were places that had never been considered by company geologists. Goldcorp took these suggestions and began drilling. The result was the astounding discovery of more than 8 million ounces of new gold reserves. Not only did the company discover the new gold, they did it record time. The collaborative process of finding it shaved two to three years off the time previously needed for exploration using established in-house procedures. The company went from a dying firm with the vultures circling overhead to a $9 billion juggernaut overnight. The key to this dramatic turnaround was the openness of the company to collaborate with many others outside the firm.

The story of Goldcorp is just one example of the kind of a new business environment that has been spawned by online digital tools that facilitate instantaneous worldwide communication, interaction, and participation. In this environment, mass collaboration is not only accepted, but also greatly valued and encouraged. So when we say that we must let students collaborate, we are not just talking about playing games. Collaboration skills are essential skills for success in the modern workplace. It is clear that online collaboration using digital tools has already become an effective way for individuals, organizations, and businesses to get work done. It is also clear that the amount of this kind of collaboration is only going to increase in the future. In light of this, it is imperative that educators ask themselves how they are going to prepare their students to work in this environment. In answering that question, we must remember that the digital generation already knows how to collaborate. They have been collaborating in the online digital world for personal and recreational reasons for much of their lives. What teachers must do is shift the collaboration the students do to include working together on joint projects that develop the kinds of skills that will help them in the new digital workplace.

Students Must Develop 21st-Century Collaboration Skills

Before we go any further, it is important that we emphasize that the kinds of joint projects we are talking about involve much more than just getting students to work together in the classroom. They must be comfortable working with someone who is not physically present in the room. We must ensure that students develop the skills needed to communicate with an online partner, exchange files with them, and do simultaneous collaborative work using a wide range of online tools that allow two or more people to work on the same digital file at the same time, whether that file contains text, images, video, or other multimedia information. The good news is that teachers don't have to abandon their curriculum to make this happen. Students can develop the 21st-century collaboration skills they need while working on digital online projects that relate to their courses, including math, English, social studies, science, or any other courses for that matter.

Collaboration can begin between students in the same class. They can be asked to meet online and use digital tools to simultaneously work on a joint project. Projects like this can begin in school, but because the tools are online, students can continue their work outside class time. In addition, teachers must actively seek out students in other schools across town, across the state or province, across the country, even across the world for the students in their classes to work with. There are many web sites that can help teacher make this happen; ePals, Telecollaborate, Global SchoolNet, and The Global Education Collaborative are just some examples of sites that facilitate virtual partners for students.

It is important that the students produce real digital work when collaborating, whether it is the creation of a web site, production of a video, participation in a blog, contribution to a wiki, publishing of a document, or completion of a presentation. Teachers must expand their idea of what school projects could be to include these and many other digital products. Students also need to learn the communication skills required to make a virtual workgroup function. They must learn how to plan joint work, to negotiate the distribution of work between group members, and to resolve conflicts. They must also learn the technical skills required to assemble the various digital components into a final product in the same way the woman in the Vancouver airport was assembling the report that was to be submitted to her boss in Denver. Teachers must spend enough time participating in a virtual collaborative working environment to be able to guide students in solving problems with digital tools and their virtual partners.

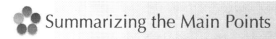

Summarizing the Main Points

- If teachers are going to connect not only with the world of their students, but also equip those students with relevant skills for their future lives, then it is critical that teachers grasp the extent that collaboration has spread across the modern world.

- By the time they have reached their teens, kids will be very comfortable interacting with and working with people online.

- Collaboration has become an indispensable method for applying the power of collective thought to create intellectual work of great value to mankind.

- Collaboration skills are essential skills for success in the modern workplace.

- Students can develop the 21st-century collaboration skills they need while working on digital online projects.

Some Questions to Consider

- How is collaboration different today than it was in the 20th century?

- How can educators prepare their students to work in the digital online environment?

- What are examples of how students are connecting digitally, and how can these be applied to the classroom?

- What are the benefits of mass collaboration?

- How can teachers incorporate collaboration into their curriculum?

Reading and References

Buck Institute For Education. (2003). *Project based learning handbook : A guide to standards-focused project-based learning for middle and high school teachers* (2nd ed.). Novato, CA.

McCain, T. (2005). *Teaching for tomorrow: Teaching content and problem-solving skills.* Thousand Oaks, CA: Corwin.

Prensky, M. (2010). *Teaching digital natives: Partnering for real learning.* Thousand Oaks, CA: Corwin.

Shirky, C. (2008). *Here comes everybody: The power of organizing with organizations.* New York: The Penguin Press.

Tapscott, D. (2008). *Wikinomics: How mass collaboration changes everything.* New York: McGraw-Hill.

Trilling, B., & Fadel, C. (2009). *21st century skills: Learning for life in our times.* San Francisco: Jossey-Bass.

Chapter 11
Teachers Must Teach Students Visually

> A visual culture is taking over the world.
>
> **John Naisbitt**

It's a visual world and people are reading less and they are reading differently. In a moment we will outline some of the major trends that are occurring that substantiate the assertions we made in the previous sentence, but before we do that, we must address the issue of the teaching of reading and writing in schools. Reading and writing are motherhood issues for parents and teachers—they are such a vital part of what everyone considers a proper education that any talk about changing anything about reading and writing instruction can be tantamount to suggesting that members of the Catholic Church stop believing in the pope. There is something sacred about teaching reading to young minds. So we want to begin this discussion of the modern communication landscape by stating very clearly that we are adamant that reading and writing must continue to be taught to all students. Reading opens up a wonderful world of imagination, deep thought, and communication of ideas that have been written by great minds from the beginning of recorded history to the present. The ability to write is a key that opens a door to a much bigger world of communication of thoughts, especially in the modern information age. Writing enables an individual to communicate with a much wider audience, both now and in the future, than could be done in any other way. Furthermore, and perhaps even more important, learning to read and write develops powerful cognitive skills that empower an individual to think logically and follow complex ideas and arguments. It is inconceivable that any thought of adequately educating young people could ever not have reading and writing instruction as a centerpiece. However, the online digital world is having a significant impact on how communication takes place in the modern world. It is important that we examine what is happening and how instruction should be adjusted to match the reality of the world students live in now and the world they will enter upon graduation and to equip them with the relevant skills they will need to be consumers and producers of information. Keeping in mind the continuing importance of students learning to read and write, let's take a look at what is happening to communication in the world.

Communication Has Gone Visual

In a word, the world of communication has gone visual. It started with the emergence of television in the 1950s and 1960s. Many people projected that this new visual medium would be the end of written communication in a very short time. While the predictions were wrong about the end of written communication, the advent of widespread television use marked a significant shift in the way the average person could get information and entertainment—a shift toward mass consumption of visual information. We began to see the emergence of a new category of reader, not illiterate, but aliterate—people who could read, but generally didn't. These people get their information about the world from the six o'clock or eleven o'clock news on television.

Another development that accompanied the emergence of television was the growth in the use of still cameras by the general public. Photography has progressed from expensive black-and-white cameras in the early part of the 20th century to color cameras in the 1950s to inexpensive cameras in the 1970s to digital cameras in the 1990s to inexpensive digital cameras in the early part of the 21st century. With each stage of development in this progression, the circle of photographers got larger. Today, with cheap digital cameras and cell phones equipped with digital cameras, photography has become ubiquitous.

> *Seemingly overnight, an entire world's worth of information became accessible through the easy-to-use interface of the web browser.*

Along with the growth in the use of cameras for still photography was the emergence of widespread use of video cameras. For the longest time, the only way to see moving pictures was at the theater. That changed in the 1950s and 1960s with the arrival of the first consumer movie cameras. While they were expensive and lacked the ability to record sound, these cameras allowed average people to record family events and tourist activities in full-motion movies. The real breakthrough in widespread movie production came in the 1980s with the development of the camcorder, a handheld camera capable of recording both moving pictures and sound. A groundbreaking feature of these camcorders was that they could be connected to a television for playback. By eliminating the need for film processing, these devices were a huge step forward in movie production by the general public. However, true widespread use of these devices happened in the 1990s and 2000s, when affordable digital video cameras became available and their movies could be downloaded directly to a computer. Not only were these devices convenient, by sending their movies to a computer, the movie clips could be edited, transitions between clips could be created, soundtracks could be added, and text effects could be superimposed over the video. Digital video editing made it possible for the average person to produce professional-quality movies that had been exclusively in the domain of professional moviemakers only a few years previous.

The watershed in the shift toward visual communication came with the rapid emergence of the World Wide Web in the mid-1990s. One of the key features of this new information and communication tool was the visual nature of the interface people used to access what they wanted to see or read. Colors, icons, and photos became as important as words in this highly interactive visual environment. The whole concept of reading was altered in this world to include all these graphical items along with words to enhance communication. In addition, the World Wide Web provided an efficient vehicle for distributing all the forms of visual communication we have just discussed. In less than 10 years since the World Wide Web exploded into the consciousness of the average person, we have seen the development of huge numbers of sites devoted to all kinds of graphics. Just to name a few: Flickr.com provides access to an incredible collection of photos, Facebook.com and MySpace.com allow people to share personal photos and videos (14 million photos are added to Facebook every day), YouTube.com allows visitors to view a staggering number of videos on just about any topic you can think of, and Craftytv.com allows people to watch television online free of charge. Today, the majority of web sites contain photos, and many contain videos. This Internet is a highly visual environment.

In 2004, Apple introduced a new form of visual communication that combined the global reach of the World Wide Web with the power of moving pictures to convey messages—podcasts. Podcasts allowed everyone with a video camera to show their movies to a global audience. These began as videos that could be viewed on the amazingly clear screens of handheld iPod devices, but soon became videos that could be played on computers and cell phones as well. Videos were soon created for lectures, meetings, how-to demonstrations, and a multitude of other movie presentations. Web sites like iTunes.com and Podcast.com give people access to podcasts covering a tremendous range of material.

The World Wide Web was responsible for another important development in the shift to a visual world. The Web brought an avalanche of information into the average person's home or place of work. When people realized how powerful the Internet was for communicating, there was a rush by individuals, businesses, educational institutions, entertainment companies, and a wide variety of organizations to get their material onto the Web. Seemingly overnight, an entire world's worth of information became accessible through the easy-to-use interface of the web browser. It is important to note that the majority of this communication that was being transferred to the Web was in textual form. The amount of information to be read on any particular topic that was available to anyone with access to the Internet went through the roof. This explosion of textual content made it impossible for anyone to keep up with the reading required to stay on top of a field of interest.

Keeping Up With the Information

The staggering amount of information available has had an interesting effect on people. There has been a marked increase in the pressure to keep up with all the information in the world, either personally or professionally. At the same time, the sheer amount of information available makes it impossible to stay on top of everything that is being written on a particular subject. People are being overwhelmed with raw data and don't have enough time to sort out what is important from what is not. Richard Saul Wurman (2002) called this condition information anxiety in a book with that same title. He describes information anxiety as "the gap between what you know and what you think you should know" (Wurman, 2002, p. 14). It is a condition that is affecting more and more people every day.

Along with the skyrocketing amount of information in the world is an increase in the pace of life. The instant world of the Web, cell phones, email, and all the other devices that give us instant feedback have created an environment where things happen much more quickly than ever before. Most people we encounter complain of having too much to do and too little time to do it. Yet the amount of information in the world has been growing exponentially due to technological development. This has created a heightened need for communication to transmit the most information possible in the least amount of time.

It is the convergence of all these factors that is creating the need for communication to shift to a visual format. Powerful yet inexpensive technology is widely available to create photos and videos. The Web is a visual environment that provides the perfect vehicle for distributing all forms of visual communication. People are experiencing increasing levels of information anxiety as the Web makes more and more information readily accessible. The pace of life has quickened with technology that gives us more and more instant communication. These factors have combined to create a pressing need to find the most efficient ways to communicate. Visual communication has been the obvious choice for a world under this kind of pressure.

Information in a visual format has great power to communicate. You know the old saying: A picture is worth a thousand words. That is precisely why so much of the communication in the modern world is going visual. Visual forms of communication convey much more information in a given period of time than traditional reading could possibly accomplish. Earlier in the book (p. 27), we cited the 3M research that indicates the brain processes visual information 60,000 times faster than it does text. According to a recent U.S. Air Force report, one-third of our brains is devoted to processing images while much less is devoted to processing words. The brain can process images so quickly that several images per second can be flashed in front of a person's eyes in rapid succession and his or her brain can still capture and remember the information contained in each picture. It is this ability of the brain to process visual information so efficiently that has made visual communication so appealing.

It's an MTV World

As we have discussed, the shift toward more visual communication began many years ago when still photography became available and affordable for the average individual. As all the factors we have presented in this chapter began to converge, the move toward more visual communication started to pick up speed. Once the Web arrived, a massive shift occurred. John Naisbitt captures the nature of this shift in the following statement:

> It is an MTV world, a world where visual narrative is overwhelming literary narrative. (Naisbitt, 2006, p. 113)

Take a look at the industry that is under the most pressure in this new online world—print-based publishing. Publications like newspapers and magazines are really feeling the pinch as they try to compete with computer-based and cell phone-based online communications—Just look at the transformation that has occurred in the appearance of these kinds of publications in the last 20 years. Publishers have responded with the use of color, photos, and graphics of all kinds to make their publications more appealing and accessible to readers who are growing more and more accustomed to visual communications. To see how far the shift to visual communication has gone, pick up a magazine like *Cosmopolitan* and take a look at the advertisements. Most of them consist of a single photograph with a small line of text that identifies the product or company sponsoring the ad. Compare this to the ads of the 1960s or 1970s, where the page contained many details about a product to promote its purchase. There has been a major rethinking of advertising as visual communication. This was highlighted in an interview John Naisbitt had with Olivero Toscani, the person responsible for marketing Luciano Benetton's Italian fashion company. Naisbitt records the following words from that interview in his book, *Mind set!: Reset Your Thinking and See the Future,* Toscani's words capture the amazing shift that has taken place in how advertisements convey their messages in the modern world.

> *The purpose of advertising is not to sell more. It's to do with institutional publicity, whose aim is to communicate the company's values. We need to convey a single strong image, which can be shared anywhere in the world.* (Naisbitt, 2006, p. 122)

But even with all their efforts to modernize their product with increased visual content, many print-based publications are losing out to the online world. Traditional newspapers, for example, are dying a slow death. In November 2007, *The New York Times* reported that readership numbers fell across the newspaper industry by 3 percent in the previous year, continuing a trend that began in the 1990s. This article about newspaper readership is significant because it details the two major aspects of the shift that is occurring in modern reading. While the readership of newspapers via traditional reading behavior is dropping, the readership of online newspapers being read with new reading behavior is rising, especially in terms of younger readers. (Editor and Publisher, October 26, 2009 - http://www.editorandpublisher.com/eandp/news/article_display.jsp?vnu_content_id=1004030291)

Evidence of just how significant the shift in reading has become came in March 2009 when the *Seattle Post Intelligencer* announced that it was ceasing to publish a print-based newspaper while it focused on its online edition. Following is a quote from an article on MSN.com that notes the importance of this decision:

> *Now the Post Intelligencer will shift entirely to the Web. . . . Hearst's decision to abandon the print product in favor of an Internet-only version is the first for a large American newspaper.*

Reading of newspapers is not the only casualty in this shift in reading behavior. Book reading is feeling the effects of this shift as well. Naisbitt tells us that after years of explosive growth, in 2006 publishers reported a drop from the previous year (Naisbitt, 2006). The bottom line is that traditional reading is declining. The National Endowment for the Arts (NEA) conducted a massive study on the reading habits of American people. It was based on a sample size of 17,000 interviews with people of all ages and a wide range of ethnic backgrounds. This study revealed that less than half of the adult American population now reads literature (NEA, 2004, p. 9). It also revealed that total book reading across all subject areas is declining significantly (NEA, 2004, p. 9). According to the study, over the decade from 1992 to 2002, reading any book declined by 7 percent, while reading literature declined by 14 percent. This decline occurred across racial lines with less reading by whites, African Americans, and Hispanics. Of great importance to educators, the report indicated that the decline in reading is most acute in young people.

> *Over the past 20 years, young adults (18–34) have declined from being those most likely to read literature to those least likely (with the exception of those age 65 and above). The rate of decline for the youngest adults (18–24) is 55 percent greater than that of the total adult population (–28 percent versus –18 percent).* (NEA, 2004, p. 11)

One of the major reasons for this more exaggerated decline of reading in young people is that they are the ones who have grown up in the digital world. They are the ones who have adopted online digital tools into their lives and accept them as normal. The authors of *Reading at Risk* comment on the competition reading faces from these new innovations.

> *The decline in reading correlates with increased participation in a variety of electronic media, including the Internet, video games, and portable digital devices. Literature now competes with an enormous array of electronic media. While no single activity is responsible for the decline of reading, the cumulative presence and availability of these alternatives have increasingly drawn Americans away from reading.* (NEA, 2004, p. 12)

The shift to visual communication is undeniable, and this shift is having a significant impact on traditional reading, especially in young people. Teachers cannot ignore what is occurring. Dealing with this change in reading behavior, however, may be quite difficult for teachers because of their personal past experience with reading. University training has inculcated a love for words and books that is deeply rooted in the paradigm teachers have for what reading is. However, communication in the world of today is not done exclusively with text. As we have noted, visual content is overwhelming textual content in the digital environment.

A new way of communicating is rapidly emerging, one that incorporates visual components along with words to convey messages more effectively for people operating in the fast-paced, time-starved modern personal and professional environment. Teachers must take notice of this important shift. Naisbitt puts it this way:

> *The history of civilization is a history of communication. If communication shifts from word to visual, we need to learn a new language to interact.* (Naisbitt, 2006, p. 117)

It is vital that we take a close look at the direction communication is heading in the modern world. Only by doing this can we sort out how to respond to this massive shift that is occurring in reading behavior. Before we discuss the nature of this shift, however, it will be helpful to distinguish between different kinds of reading.

Types of Reading

There are three main types of reading. The first is what we will call functional reading. This is the reading we do every day in order to function in the world. Functional reading enables a person to navigate to a destination, make a purchasing decision, or accomplish a task. This is reading with a specific short-term goal in mind. It involves reading signs, instructions, the ingredients in foods, letters and email, recipes, the specifications for products, the show times for movies, and so on.

The second type of reading is reading for enlightenment and enrichment. This is reading that we do to learn something new about current events, sports, politics, business, entertainment, history, science, music, and so on. Enrichment comes from reading material that gives meaning to life by reading about religion, philosophy, and self-help material. Strong personal interest motivates this kind of reading. We read newspapers, magazines, and nonfiction books when we are reading for enlightenment and enrichment.

The third type of reading is reading for entertainment and leisure. This is reading of literature. This reading takes the reader into the world of imagination and fantasy. For this kind of reading, we read short stories, novels, poems, and plays. Personal interest also motivates this kind of reading.

These are not hard and fast categories, and there is overlap in the distinctions we have made between the different kinds of reading. For example, someone might read nonfiction books that provide enlightenment for entertainment. Reading short sections of a manual is functional reading, but reading a book that provides more detailed coverage is reading for enlightenment. Reading in school is supposed to be reading for enlightenment and entertainment, but it is most often just functional reading because personal interest is missing and the focus for the student is on completing a task just to get a grade. However, although there are some fuzzy edges between them, these general distinctions will be helpful when discussing the impact the modern world is having on reading behavior.

Functional reading has been significantly influenced by the shift to visual communication. Take modern signs, for example. Words have been replaced by icons and symbols on everything from road signs to washroom signs. Instructions for assembly of products bought from stores like Ikea or connection instructions for electronic products now contain more illustrations and photos than text. For the majority of people, especially young people, information has gone online. This is a visual world where visual clues are almost always given to assist a person with navigation and to identify content. Color, icons, photos, and animation are used liberally in this environment. Words are still used, of course, but their role is much more limited than in pre-digital days. Daily online interpersonal communication is still done primarily using text, but the messages are usually done in short bursts of words. Email messages are often short and do not follow the rules of spelling and grammar. Messages sent by Twitter on the Web or by texting on cell phones are usually very short and use an abbreviated form of word spelling to convey meaning in the fewest keystrokes or thumb presses as possible.

Reading for enlightenment has also been greatly affected by the move of information to the Web. Reading for learning about a topic of interest is quite different in this online world. It is interactive and the user gets to choose what to see, where to go, and what to read. Written content is often broken into chunks so as not to overwhelm the reader with long passages of text that look like too much work to read. Reading is done in a kind of a staccato pattern of scanning the screen for links and reading short passages of text looking for personal relevance, and then moving on quickly to another activity. People simply don't read long passages of text like they used to. It's more like commando reading—go in and look for key words or phrases that will get the meaning of a message quickly and then move on. In addition, you will often find that in the online digital world, stories are told, points of view are explained, events are reported, and feelings conveyed via photos, videos, and audio narration without requiring a person to read any text at all. Reading in games often follows a very similar pattern. The person playing the game looks for visual clues, short phrases, or single words that can be used to make decisions for completing the game. Instructions are most often provided in point form. Often instructions are spoken to the game player as he or she explores the visual environment of the game.

> *Reading for learning about a topic of interest is quite different in this online world. It is interactive and the user gets to choose what to see, where to go, and what to read.*

The reading habits picked up in the online digital world transfer to reading traditional paper-based material when people are reading for enlightenment. The digital generation scans pages for keywords or phrases, they look for visual clues that will assist with finding the meaning of a message quickly, and they skip long passages of text completely. In some ways, this is not really that dissimilar to the kind of reading that people have always done. They have always wanted to cut to the chase, to get to the meaning quickly. That is why most people only read the executive summaries of reports and they buy Cliff Notes/Coles Notes—they want to get to the heart of a message without wading through all the superfluous material. This kind of reading behavior has been exaggerated in the digital world, and the digital generation wants to read all material this way.

Reading for entertainment and leisure has been a casualty in this shift in reading behavior in the modern world. As we mentioned above, this kind of reading is facing stiff competition from a number of other activities. Modern readers, especially young modern readers, are finding other things to do with their time than read short stories and novels. Young adults have gone from being the most likely to read literature to being the least likely to do so.

What Can Educators Do?

So what does all this mean for teachers? There are three responses that we must consider. First, we must counterbalance the shift away from reading books by redoubling our efforts to foster a love for reading literature. As professional educators, we must look very critically at the current focus in schools on test scores because that focus is a major factor in the decline in reading literature by young people. In an article for *The Independent*, education correspondent Sarah Cassidy reports on a study by the English educational watchdog Ofsted that explored the reasons for the decline in reading by young people. They interviewed a wide range of teachers about the reading that was done in their classrooms. Teachers reported that the pressure to raise test scores negatively affected the amount and the kind of reading that they did with their students:

> *Many teachers no longer read poems or stories to their class because they feel guilty that they are wasting valuable teaching time.* (Cassidy, 2005)

Traditional reading of literature is simply too important to abandon. For students, this kind of reading can provide a welcome break from the tedium of preparing for tests. The world of stories can add great interest to the school experience, as can reading for enlightenment. These types of reading can connect a young reader with his or her culture, acquaint him or her with the historical roots of what we see in the world today, foster deep thought about a wide range of topics, open up a wonderful world of fantasy and imagination, and train the mind to follow a story or an idea that takes time to develop. We simply must find ways to include activities that inculcate a love for reading in the midst of the other activities targeted at boosting test scores.

Second, we must teach students visually. This is really not a new idea. Kindergarten and primary teachers have always been teaching this way. They use illustrations, shapes, color, and photos to convey meaning to their students. But the use of visuals begins to decline as students move into the intermediate grades and continues to decline through junior and senior high school. We must find ways to include visuals in our teaching as students go further in school. This is a tightrope that we must walk. On one side, we have the need to engage the digital generation in the learning in the classroom. On the other side, we have the need to cover the material in our courses. But as we mentioned earlier, with high numbers of students who are dropping out of school and even more who are disinterested in the instruction they are encountering, it is critical that we make engagement a priority.

We must stand back and look at how the world of school is different from the world students experience outside the classroom. Our focus in this chapter has been on the shift to visual communication that has occurred and is continuing to occur in the world today. As we have mentioned, one of the prime reasons for this shift is that visual communication can convey much more information to a person in a short period of time than other forms of communication. Now teaching is based on communication. If we can communicate, then students can learn. If we don't communicate or we communicate the wrong message, then students lose interest or they become misinformed. Any change in the way communication occurs with our students is of vital importance to us as educators. If the world has learned a new visual language for communicating, then it is critical that we not only learn that language, but also use it to keep our instruction effective in the modern environment. Further, there may be great benefits in terms of enhanced communication by using this new visual language in our teaching. Exploring the use of any improvements that can help us communicate better must be a professional imperative.

Teaching has long been based on teachers talking while students listen and take notes. Students have also been expected to read material that supports the direct classroom teaching. This paradigm for instruction dates back to the ancient Greeks in the time of Aristotle. This has certainly been the main paradigm for teaching for the majority of classrooms throughout the 20th century. This model of students listening to teachers talking and students reading supporting textual information is so pervasive that this approach is taken for granted by most teachers, especially if they teach higher up in the school system.

But as we have just discussed, the world students experience away from school is highly visual. It is a world of online information of photos and videos, a world of games, watching television and DVDs, and growing fast is the downloading of movies to computers, cell phones, iPods, and similar devices for viewing when convenient. This communication involves much less traditional reading than ever before. The students arriving in our classrooms are not the readers the system was designed for, nor are they the readers most teachers have been trained to teach. They come equipped with a new set of skills that enable them to process visual information much more effectively than text. They are accustomed to receiving this visual information in a highly interactive environment where they have control of the direction and the pace of the experience. Asking these students to sit while teachers talk or to do the traditional reading of long passages of uninterrupted text is like trying to fit a round peg in a square hole.

It is important for teachers to honestly assess the kind of learning experience students are receiving in their classrooms. Does it fit with the modern world? Will students feel that the way they are learning is relevant to the online visual world that awaits them when school is over? How can we adjust our instruction to include the visual presentation of information that will match the world students live in? And most important, how can we use the visual presentation of information to improve communication over nonvisual methods?

The majority of teachers who have incorporated new media into their instruction have largely grafted the new tools onto an old approach to teaching.

What we are advocating is a significant shift in the thinking around how communication takes place in teaching that goes well beyond what is occurring now. The majority of teachers who have incorporated new media into their instruction have largely grafted the new tools onto an old approach to teaching. Take web sites, for example. Although a growing number of teachers are now maintaining their own web sites using widely available online tools or using the tools on school district Moodle servers, often much of the information on those sites is textual with long passages of uninterrupted text with no hyperlinked subsections. More important, the material on the sites, whether textual or visual, is supplemental to the instruction in the classroom. Teachers continue to teach largely the way they did before they had a web site with a great deal of their instruction involving talking to students. What we are saying is that a new medium like the World Wide Web should be used as the primary method for communication at least part of the time in the classroom. The new medium should be used to communicate material central to a course instead of talking to students or traditional reading. Further, the design of any web site used in this manner must capitalize on the potential for effective visual communication.

In his book, *Understanding Media: The Extensions of Man*, Marshall McLuhan wrote:

> *The medium is the message.* (McLuhan, 1964, p. 7)

McLuhan understood that new electronic media would have an enormous impact on communication. He wrote this in 1964. His prescient statement highlights the powerful role new media has to influence our lives, and the statement is all that more profound in the modern world of compelling new visual media. It is time that educators embrace the implications of McLuhan's insight in how they teach.

Third, we must teach students how to construct effective visual communication. There are two aspects to providing students with instruction on how effective visual communication is created. Students must be equipped with an understanding of how their perceptions can be manipulated in visual communication because they are consumers of visual information. Young people need to be given knowledge and guidance in how to discern what is really being said in visual communication. As consumers of visual messages from a very young age, our students must be given the understanding necessary to correctly interpret what is being conveyed visually. Without this understanding, they are ripe for receiving biased and even blatantly misleading messages through visual manipulation from advertisers, political parties, religious groups, minority groups with some sort of agenda, and a wide variety of groups on the fringe of society. Currently, students do not receive this kind of instruction on how visual communication works until high school, and then only if they choose to take an elective course on graphics, if it is offered at their school. However, understanding visual manipulation is far too important only to be offered to so few students and so late in their school lives. This understanding is a critical part of being literate in the modern visual world. It must be taught to students from an early age.

Our students are also producers of visual information. They have access to widely available inexpensive digital tools that let them create desktop published documents, web sites, blogs, wikis, videos, photos, podcasts, and a whole host of other means of visual communication. In *Here Comes Everybody*, Clay Shirky (2008) calls this the mass amateurization of communication, which sounds like a good thing. However, there are two sides to this development. On the one hand, this represents a wonderful new world of freedom for any individual to create forms of visual communication that were previously only available to a very small group of well-funded professionals. On the other hand, this mass amateurization of communication has allowed untrained people to create a lot of truly horrible visual information that is not effective at conveying its message at all. Now that these very powerful tools have been placed in the hands of the general public, average individuals need to be trained on how to use them effectively.

Our students need the technical skills to operate equipment like cameras, but they usually pick up those skills very quickly once they get their hands on a device. What they really need, what anyone trying to communicate visually needs, are the empowering principles of visual image construction. These principles include graphic design, the effective use of color, principles of effective photography, and principles of effective movie making.

Summarizing the Main Points

- The online digital world is having a significant impact on how communication takes place in the modern world.

- There has been a marked increase in the pressure to keep up with all the information available in the world today.

- It is vital that we take a close look at the direction communication is heading in the modern world.

- Visual communication can convey much more information to a person in a short period of time than other forms of communication.

- We must teach students visually and teach them how to construct effective visual communication.

Some Questions to Consider

- How has communication changed in the 21st century?

- What is information anxiety?

- What are the different types of reading, and how have they been affected by the digital world?

- How can educators counterbalance the shift away from traditional reading? Is traditional reading still important?

- Why should educators teach students the principles of visual image construction?

Reading and References

Burmark, L. (2002). *Visual literacy: Learn to see, see to learn*. New York: ASCD.

Cassidy, S. (2005). Tests blamed for decline of reading for pleasure. *The Independent,* October 5. Retrieved www.independent.co.uk/news/education/education-news/tests-blamed-for-decline-of-reading-for-pleasure-509626.html

Editor and Publisher, October 26, 2009 www.editorandpublisher.com/eandp/news/article_display.jsp?vnu_content_id=1004030291

McLuhan, M. (1964). *Understanding media—The extensions of man*. Boston: MIT Press.

Medina, J. (2008). *Brain rules: 12 principles for surviving and thriving at work, home, and school*. Seattle, WA: Pear Press.

Naisbitt, J. (2006). *Mind set!: Reset your thinking and see the future*. New York: HarperBusiness.

National Endowment for the Arts. (2004). *Reading at Risk: A survey of literary reading in America*. Washington, DC: Author.

Seattle Post Intelligencer, March 17, 2009, www.seattlepi.com/business/403793_piclosure17.html

Shirky, C. (2008). *Here comes everybody: The power of organizing with organizations*. New York: The Penguin Press.

Tapscott, D. (2009). *Grown up digital: How the net generation is changing your world*. New York: McGraw-Hill.

Trilling, B., & Fadel, C. (2009). *21st century skills: Learning for life in our times*. San Francisco: Jossey-Bass.

Wurman, R.S. (2002). *Information anxiety*. New York: Hayden.

Chapter 12
Teachers Must Re-Evaluate Evaluation

> We must broaden our concept of testing to include assessments based on long-term interdisciplinary projects—in other words, on something bearing a resemblance to reality.
>
> **David Thornburg**

As any teacher will tell you, in education the evaluative tail wags the instructional dog. Evaluation has a profound impact on how teachers teach and what students learn. Every teacher has run into the following question when having a class discussion: "Is this going to be on the test?"

It is the most logical question a student can ask because it gets straight to the bottom line for their learning—it tells them whether to pay attention or not, and whether this new information will affect them or not. If the material is going to be on the test (or evaluated in some other way), then the next question is: "How much is it worth?"

Students intuitively know what is important in a class by the value of the mark that the teacher assigns to material to be learned. It is a truism of life that the value of things determines what a person focuses on and how much effort they are willing to put into getting it. It is true for students when they decide what to focus on when they learn and it is true for teachers when they determine what their instruction will focus on when they deliver their lessons. Evaluation is so inextricably linked to instruction and learning that you must view them as one.

Performance Assessment Must Change

We believe that the way performance is assessed in school must change. Some educators have asked us, "Why?" This book is our response. The world has changed, kids have changed, and the knowledge and skills needed for success in the world have changed. That means instruction has to change. And if we hope to change instruction, we must change evaluation. Any attempts to significantly shift what teachers and students do must focus on evaluation.

What about evaluation needs to be different? To answer this, we must consider what we have been talking about throughout this book. We have outlined that people in the modern world need different abilities to adequately function in a high-tech world and use the online digital tools that are central to digital culture. This means that the notion of literacy has changed for the world of the 21st century. It is certain that what it means to be literate will look different than it did only a few years ago, and certainly a world away from what it did when many parents, teachers, administrators, community members, and politicians grew up.

That's a huge problem when it comes to changing evaluation of ability in school. The new knowledge and skills that students have today in many cases don't look like the knowledge and skills that adults today needed when they grew up. The knowledge and skills we need to teach students to prepare them for their future are even more foreign. This is a challenge not only for instruction, but also for evaluation because our past experience makes it difficult, or even impossible, to see the value in new ways of doing things. And we can't evaluate what we don't see. Let us explain.

Most adults involved in the school system today grew up in the 20th century and virtually all adults involved in the school system today, even our youngest teachers, attended schools that had a 20th-century approach to teaching and learning. This experience created a mindset for what we value in school. It is this 20th-century mindset that is the major obstacle when trying to develop an evaluation scheme for 21st-century knowledge and skills. In fact, this mindset can actually prevent us from seeing what is staring us in the face. Let us illustrate this point with an example from the 1970s. There is a well-known story of what happened to the Swiss watch-making industry when digital watches were invented. Prior to that invention, the Swiss controlled more than 85 percent of the production of the world's fine watches. And because watches had looked the same for hundreds of years, there was an established mindset for what a watch looked like.

Along comes the digital watch, which would explode onto the market and displace the vast majority of watch production in just a few short years. How did the Swiss respond to this invention? Astonishingly, they did nothing. And by the time they realized that they had missed the boat, it was too late for their industry. Almost all of the Swiss watchmakers lost their jobs in less than a two-year span.

The point of this story is that even though we understand in retrospect that the digital watch was the future of the watch-making industry, the Swiss watchmakers couldn't see what was staring them in the face. They had a long-established mindset of what a watch was—and to them, digital watches were not real watches. They were so locked into one way of thinking that they couldn't see things from another perspective. And that mindset cost them dearly.

Teachers are in much the same position today. Instruction and learning have been the same for a long time—in fact, for more than a hundred years. There is a long-established mindset for what learning looks like and how it is evaluated. But now due in large part to new technological developments, we are in times of rapid change. The way the new digital world operates has radically redefined much of the essential knowledge and skills students need to function in life. We are seeing students arrive at school with a radically different life experience and a substantially different skill set than ever before.

How will we respond? Will we see these new skills that are staring us in the face and, just like the Swiss watchmakers, will our mindset make us say these aren't real skills because they don't look like the ones we're used to? Or will we recognize the value of what kids are able to do and see the need for adjusting not only what we teach them and how we teach them, but also the need for adjusting the way we evaluate their performance at school?

Mindsets Must Change

The biggest issue we face in shifting evaluation of students is changing the long-standing mindset that teachers, administrators, parents, community members, and politicians have for what knowledge and skills should be valued in school. Until that issue is dealt with, adults will look at the digital generation, but not see the skills and knowledge they have. Nor will they see the skills and knowledge these kids will need for their future life. They will continue to focus on the traditional skills that they learned when they were in school because they have served them well. They will continue to use 20th-century evaluative tools that measure 20th-century skills and, in doing so, do a terrific job of preparing students for a world that no longer exists. The adults involved in the school system today must open their eyes to the realities of 21st-century digital culture and business practice.

Now let us be clear. We are in no way saying that all knowledge and skills that have been traditionally taught in school are now obsolete. Many of the things that were taught throughout the 20th century remain valid today, some even more so. But as we mentioned earlier in the book, teachers must understand that there has been a shift in emphasis in what is required for success, and a different skill set is needed to function in a digital world. Earlier, we outlined the following new basic skills:

Changing instruction to focus on these 21st-century fluencies will have two significant impacts on evaluation. First, these new fluency and thinking skills are process skills, not content skills. They equip students with a process that can be applied over and over again as they progress through their lives.

Process skills are the most powerful skills we can teach our students. We have always known the power of process skills—that is exactly what we are teaching students when we teach them to read and write. We don't teach them how to read a single page, we teach them the process of reading to empower them to read magazines, cereal boxes, product instructions, web sites, and books we never dreamed of when we started. Similarly, we don't teach them to write a single paragraph, we teach them the process of writing so they can go on to write essays, stories, reports, articles, and books that we had no idea of when we began. This is the power of process in learning—it starts a wonderful journey for a young mind because it gives them wings to fly wherever they choose to go.

Process skills are difficult to assess using traditional evaluation tools. They are hard to measure on a pencil-and-paper test, and particularly with multiple-choice tests. That doesn't mean they can't be measured, but a shift in how it's done is required. Evaluation strategies for assessing a student's progress in acquiring process skills can be found in both *Teaching for Tomorrow* (McCain, 2005) and the *Project Based Learning Handbook* (Buck Institute for Education, 2003).

Teaching for Tomorrow outlines a problem-solving process called the 4Ds, which empowers students to do the higher-level thinking needed to solve problems independently. Ted tells teachers the kinds of things to look for as students develop their abilities to apply the 4Ds to the tasks they are given. In the *Project Based Learning Handbook*, teachers are given sample rubrics that can be used to assess the development of process skills in students.

Second, changing instruction to focus on 21st-century fluency and thinking skills means there will be a shift from traditional expressions of learning to digital expressions of learning. This shift mirrors an amazing transformation that has occurred in the way people communicate information in the modern world. One of the most remarkable developments resulting from the use of online digital tools has been the ability of the average person to create communications that were previously only produced by highly trained professionals outfitted with very expensive equipment.

Now anyone can produce a movie with video and text effects, or a high-quality, multitrack sound recording, or a full-color printed publication. Furthermore, the Internet allows anyone to reach a global audience though web sites and blogs. As we discussed previously, documents like wikis are now storing valid intellectual information that has wide use for personal and professional research.

Expressions of Learning Must Change

Clay Shirky (2008) calls this transformation "mass amateurization." Mass amateurization is affecting everyone. Personal publishing and personal creativity have gone multimedia and have acquired a global reach in the 21st century. So, too, have business communications and marketing.

It is our job as teachers to prepare our students to function in this world. That will mean expecting students to produce these kinds of multimedia communications in school. It will also mean that we must develop an evaluation scheme that correctly assesses the learning students have done in creating these new multimedia communications.

This presents another challenge for adult teachers who grew up before mass amateurization occurred. Our experiences growing up involved handwritten reports and essays. Color meant using pencil crayons, even for work done in university. Multimedia meant our report had a diagram or chart that was likely photocopied. Multitrack sound recordings were only done by record companies. Movies with special effects for video and text were only done by professionals at TV stations and big movie producers like MGM, Paramount, and Warner Bros. Large collections of intellectual information were only produced by companies like Encyclopedia Britannica and World Book.

Consequently, publishing a blog or creating a video are not the first things that come to mind for most teachers when planning projects for their classes. But if we are going to prepare our students for success in the world of today and the world of tomorrow, then we must include new digital expressions of learning in the things we ask students to do in school.

Again, we are not saying that traditional expressions of learning like reports and essays no longer have a place in learning. For example, even in the 21st century, students still benefit greatly from the thinking required to develop the logic to support an argument in an essay. What we are saying is that the expression of that thinking may be something other than black words typed on white paper.

Here is a story from Ted's high school that illustrates what we are talking about when we say that new digital tools can change the expression of learning and what that means for the teacher.

One of Ted's long-time colleagues at Maple Ridge Secondary was an English teacher named Mike Josiah. Mike was the English department head at the school. He was a master teacher of great intelligence and a forward thinker. He and Ted would often have discussions about the role of technology in education. In one of those conversations in the early 1990s, Ted began talking about the capabilities of new desktop publishing tools. Mike was intrigued by the potential these tools had to enhance the teaching of the writing process in his classes. As an English teacher, he was well aware that the writing process has five steps— plan, draft, revise, proof, and publish. Mike was also aware that the publish step was the weakest part of teaching his students to write because they did not have access to the advanced tools required to publish anything more than handwritten documents. He was intrigued by the power of the word processor and the page layout program to empower his students to publish their work. He realized that his students would still have to go through all the academic rigor necessary to research, plan, and edit their writing, but he also realized that the final product they produced would look different than anything students in his classes had ever done before.

One example came to Mike's mind immediately. Instead of a traditional essay, students would now be able to produce a magazine using desktop publishing tools. The new publication could have all the intellectual work he previously required of his students, but they would take on a new format. The handwritten essays would be replaced with published articles expressing opinions on the role of the state in the life of the individual as portrayed by George Orwell in the novel *1984*. Plus, Mike saw that in addition to the writing, the publication could have images and other graphics. As his mind raced through the new possibilities, he realized that these new publishing capabilities would mean he had to acquire new skills and knowledge in order to be able to guide his students in the appropriate use of the tools and to correctly assess the work they had done with them. Although he acknowledged that this would require some work on his part, he saw the use of desktop publishing tools as a great way to add excitement and relevance to the teaching of writing in his classes.

If Mike were teaching today, he would be wrestling with a whole host of new ways for students to communicate what they have learned—web sites, blogs, wikis, podcasts, mashups, and videos, just to name a few. Teachers today have been presented with an explosion of ways for students to express what they have learned. Many of these communication tools are very new and we are challenged with the task of keeping up. However, the possibilities these new tools bring to learning have so much potential to add relevance and engagement for the digital generation that we cannot ignore them. If we are going to include them in the things we ask students to do, then we are going to have to learn how they work so we can effectively evaluate the work our students do with them.

Summarizing the Main Points

- It is the 20th-century mindset that is the major obstacle when trying to develop an evaluation scheme for 21st-century knowledge and skills.

- Educators need to recognize the value of what this generation is able to do and see the need for adjusting not only what we teach them and how we teach them, but also the need for adjusting the way we evaluate their performance at school.

- We must develop an evaluation scheme that correctly assesses the learning students have done in creating new multimedia communications.

- If we are going to prepare our students for success in the world of today and the world of tomorrow, then we must include new digital expressions of learning in the things we ask students to do in school.

- The possibilities new digital tools bring to learning have so much potential to add relevance and engagement for the digital generation that we cannot ignore them.

Some Questions to Consider

- How does evaluation need to change to fit the needs of today's students?

- What influence will changing instruction to focus on 21st-century skills have on evaluation?

- What is mass amateurization and how does it affect evaluation?

- How can traditional expressions of learning incorporate new expressions of learning?

- What is the role of technology in education? How has that changed in the 21st century?

Reading and References

Anderson, L., & Krathwohl, D. (2001). *A taxonomy for learning, teaching and assessing—A revision of Bloom's taxonomy of educational objectives*: New York: Longman.

Buck Institute for Education. (2003). *Project based learning handbook : A guide to standards-focused project-based learning for middle and high school teachers* (2nd ed.). Novato, CA.

Dryden, G., & Vos, J. (2009). *Unlimited: The new learning revolution and the seven keys to unlock it.* Auckland, New Zealand: The Learning Web.

Gardner, H. (1983). *Frames of mind: Theories of multiple intelligences.* New York: Basic Books.

McCain, T. (2005). *Teaching for tomorrow: Teaching content and problem-solving skills.* Thousand Oaks, CA: Corwin.

Medina, J. (2008). *Brain rules: 12 principles for surviving and thriving at work, home, and school.* Seattle, WA: Pear Press.

Pink, D. (2005). *A whole new mind: Moving from the information age to the conceptual age.* New York: Riverhead.

Prensky, M. (2010). *Teaching digital natives: Partnering for real learning.* Thousand Oaks, CA: Corwin.

Shirky, C. (2008). *Here comes everybody: The power of organizing with organizations.* New York: The Penguin Press.

Trilling, B., & Fadel, C. (2009). *21st century skills: Learning for life in our times.* San Francisco: Jossey-Bass.

Chapter 13

A Need for Leadership

> The growth and development of people is the highest calling of leadership.
>
> **Harvey S. Fireston**

Leadership Is Critical

Leadership is desperately needed in education today to bring about the shift in instruction that is urgently required to keep students engaged in learning and to prepare them for success in the future. It will require courage to take the leadership that is needed because leading education into the 21st century will mean going against the grain with fellow educators. It will mean going against the long-standing mindset for what teaching and learning looks like by diving into the new digital world to gain the experience needed to critically assess the value of new ways to communicate with others, to entertain ourselves, to perform work both by ourselves and collaboratively with others, and to assess the relative value of new online digital experiences with traditional nondigital ones.

The leadership that is needed will recognize that until we add the balance to our adult lives with experience in the online digital world, we will have little credibility to stand in front of our digital generation clientele and tell them we understand how to teach them for success in the modern world. This will mean upsetting the status quo that many involved in education have found so comfortable for so long. Those educators taking leadership in shifting education to a 21st-century approach will have to have a clear vision of why this shift is necessary, because steps to modify what teachers do will draw the ire of those who are unwilling to embrace change in their role.

But leading education into the 21st century will also mean at least partially going against the grain with students as well. It will mean making the digital generation turn off their digital devices once in a while. They will complain, of course, but kids will realize that their teachers are drawing from personal experience in the digital world to ensure that they have the best instructional approach. That experience in the digital world will enable teachers to know both the good and the bad of digital culture, so they can lead young people into the positive aspects of digital culture while guiding them away from the negative ones. That personal experience in digital culture will also result in knowing when to use nondigital tools to guide students into nondigital experiences that will develop truly balanced and well-rounded young individuals.

There is a great challenge before us as teachers at the beginning of the 21st century—to enter the digital world to regain the balance needed in our lives to be able to credibly lead our students into learning that will be effective for their lives in the modern world. How often have we said to our students, take control of your lives, go find out what opportunities are out in the world so you can make good choices, and then go make it happen. *Carpe diem*—seize the day! The tables have been turned, and now we are the ones faced with the challenge of seizing the day. There is a whole new world out there in the 21st century, and we need to go out and find the wonderful potential and the ugly dark side so we can make good choices in what and how we teach young minds.

Summarizing the Main Points

- Many adults live very unbalanced lives, and unless they counterbalance their old nondigital life experiences with new digital experiences, it will have catastrophic consequences for education.

- Leadership is desperately needed in education today to bring about the shift in instruction that is urgently required to keep students engaged in learning and to prepare them for success in the future.

- Leadership will mean upsetting the status quo by increasingly using online digital tools to equip students with the skills they will need to thrive in the world of the 21st century.

- Leadership will also mean going against the grain with students by telling them to turn off their digital tools so they can develop the nondigital skills that will bring balance to their lives.

Some Questions to Consider

- What can educators do to encourage the digital generation to balance virtual relationships with face-to-face relationships?

- How can educators incorporate strategies to help students develop single-tasking skills?

- What can adults do to balance traditional thinking with the digital world?

- What must leaders do to change the long-standing mindset of what teaching and learning look like in the new digital world?

Reading and References

Christensen, C., Horn, M., & Johnson, C. (2008). *Disrupting class: How disruptive innovation will change the way the world learns.* New York: McGraw-Hill.

Johnson, S. (2005). *Everything bad is good for you: How today's popular culture is actually making us smarter.* New York: Riverhead.

Medina, J. (2008). *Brain rules: 12 principles for surviving and thriving at work, home, and school.* Seattle: Pear Press.

Pink, D. (2005). *A whole new mind: Moving from the information age to the conceptual age.* New York: Riverhead.

Prensky, M. (2010). *Teaching digital natives: Partnering for real learning.* Thousand Oaks, CA: Corwin.

Small, G., & Vorgon, G. (2008). *iBrain: Surviving the technological alteration of the modern mind.* New York: Harper Collins.

Tapscott, D. (2009). *Grown up digital: How the net generation is changing your world.* New York: McGraw-Hill.

Willingham, D. (2009). *Why don't students like school? A cognitive scientist answers questions about how the mind works and what it means for the classroom.* San Francisco: John Wiley and Sons.

Bibliography

Anderson, L., & Krathwohl, D. (2001). *A taxonomy for learning, teaching and assessing—A revision of Bloom's taxonomy of educational objectives*. New York: Longman.

Bauerlein, M. (2008). *The dumbest generation: How the digital age stupefies young Americans and jeopardizes our future (Or, don't trust anyone under 30)*. New York: Tarcher.

Buck Institute for Education. (2003). *Project Based Learning Handbook: A guide to standards-focused project-based learning for middle and highs school teachers* (2nd ed.). Novato, CA.

Burmark, L. (2002). *Visual literacy: Learn to see, see to learn*. New York: ASCD.

Buskist, W., & Davis, W., (2008). *Handbook of the teaching of psychology*. Malden, MA: Blackwell Publishing.

Byerly, G., Holmes, J., Robins, D., Zang, Y., & Salaba, A. (2006,). *The "eyes" have it—Eye-tracking and usability study of schoolrooms. SirsiDynix OneSource (2)*, 6. Kent State University School of Library and Information Science.

Canton, J. (2006). *The extreme future: The top trends that will reshape the world for the next 5, 10, and 20 years*. New York: Penguin.

Carter, R. (2009). *The human brain book: An illustrated guide to its structure, function and disorders*. London: Dorling Kindersley.

Cassidy, S. (2005). Tests blamed for decline of reading for pleasure. *The Independent,* October 5. Retrieved www.independent.co.uk/news/education/education-news/tests-blamed-for-decline-of-reading-for-pleasure-509626.html

Chechik, G., Meilijson, I., & Ruppin, E. (1999). *Neuronal Regulation: A Mechanism for Synaptic Pruning During Brain Maturation. (Volume 11 , Issue 8.)* Cambridge, MA: MIT Press.

Christensen, C., Horn, M., & Johnson, C. (2008). *Disrupting class: How disruptive innovation will change the way the world learns*. New York: McGraw-Hill.

Crossman, W. (2004). *VIVO: The coming age of talking computers*. Oakland, CA: Regent Press.

DeMott, S., & Lynch, K. (2004). *Defining paternity leave: Shifting roles, new responsibilities in the family and the workplace* Menlo Park, CA: Kaiser Family Foundation.

Doidge, N. (2007). *The brain that changes itself: Stories of personal triumph from the frontiers of brain science*. New York: Penguin.

Dryden, G., & Vos, J. (2009). *Unlimited: The new learning revolution and the seven keys to unlock it*. Auckland, New Zealand: The Learning Web.

Feinstein, S. (2004). *Secrets of the teenage brain: Research-based strategies for reaching and teaching today's adolescents*. San Diego, CA: The Brain Store.

Friedman, T. (2005). *The world is flat: A brief history of the twenty-first century*. New York: Farrar, Straus and Giroux.

Friedman, T. (2008). *Hot, flat, and crowded: Why we need a green revolution and how it can renew America*. New York: Farrar, Straus and Giroux.

Gardner, H. (1983). *Frames of mind: Theories of multiple intelligences*. New York: Basic Books.

Garreau, J. (2005). *Radical evolution: The promise and peril of enhancing our minds, bodies-and what it means to be human*. New York: Random House.

Glasser, W. (1998). *The quality school*. New York: Harper.

Goodstein, A. (2007). *Totally wired: What teens and tweens are really doing online*. New York: St. Martin's Griffin.

Hirsch, E. D. (1988). *Cultural literacy: What every American needs to know*. New York: Vintage Books.

Holmqvist, K. and Wartenberg, C. (2005). *The role of local design factors for newspaper reading behaviour – an eye-tracking perspective*. Lund University Cognitive Studies, LUCS 127 ISSN 1101-8453

Hutchison, D. (2007). *Playing to learn: Video games in the classroom*. Westport, CT: Teacher Ideas Press.

Jensen, E. (2008). Super Teaching: Over 1000 Practical Strategies. p.42. Thousand Oaks, CA: Corwin Press.

Johnson, S. (2005). *Everything bad is good for you: How today's popular culture is actually making us smarter*. New York: Riverhead.

Jukes, I., McCain, T., & Crockett L. (2010). *Literacy is not enough: 21st century fluencies for the digital age*. Kelowna, BC: 21st Century Fluency Project.

Jukes, I., McCain, T., & Crockett L. (2010). *Living on the future edge: The impact of global exponential trends on education in the 21st century*. Kelowna, BC: 21st Century Fluency Project.

Kandel, E. (2006). *In search of memory: The emergence of a new science of mind*. London: W.W. Norton.

Kelly, F., McCain, T., & Jukes, I. (2008). *Teaching the digital generation: No more cookie-cutter high schools*. Thousand Oaks, CA: Corwin.

Kolb, L. (2008). *Toys to tools: Connecting student cell phones to education*. Eugene, OR: ISTE.

Kurzweil, R. (2005). *The singularity is near: When humans transcend biology*. New York: Viking Press.

Longstaff, H. (1949). *Review of attention and interest factors in advertising*. Journal of Applied Psychology. Vol 33(3), Jun 1949, pages 286-287.

McCain, T. (2005). *Teaching for tomorrow: Teaching content and problem-solving skills*. Thousand Oaks, CA: Corwin.

McCain, T., & Jukes, I. (2000). *Windows on the future: Education in the age of technology*.

Thousand Oaks, CA: Corwin.

McLuhan, M. (1964). *Understanding media: The extensions of man*. Boston: MIT Press.

Medina, J. (2008). *Brain rules: 12 principles for surviving and thriving at work, home, and school*. Seattle, WA: Pear Press.

Naisbitt, J. (2006). *Mind set!: Reset your thinking and see the future*. New York: HarperBusiness.

Nielsen, J. (2006). Jakob Nielsen's Alertbox, April 17, 2006: *F-shaped pattern for reading web content*. http://www.useit.com/alertbox/reading_pattern.html

Nielsen, J. and Loranger, H. (2006). *Prioritizing web usability*. Berkley: New Riders Press

Nielson, J. and Pernice, K. (2010). *Eyetracking web usability*. Berkley: New Riders Press

Neisser, U., & Hyman, Y. (1999). *Memory Observed: Remembering in Natural Contexts*. (2nd Edition). New York: Worth Publishing.

Nussbaum, P., & Daggett, W. (2008). *What brain research teaches us about rigor, relevance, and relationships—And what it teaches us about keeping your own brain healthy*. Rexford, NY: International Center for Leadership in Education.

Penn, W. (1956). *Research in marketing*.The Journal of Marketing, Vol. 21, No. 2 pages 200-228. American Marketing Association. http://www.jstor.org/stable/1247344

Pink, D. (2001). *Free agent nation—The future of working for yourself*. Chicago: Business Plus.

Pink, D. (2005). *A whole new mind: Moving from the information age to the conceptual age*. New York: Riverhead.

Poole, A., Ball, L. J., and Phillips, P. (2004). *In search of salience: A response time and eye movement analysis of bookmark recognition*. In S. Fincher, P. Markopolous, D. Moore, & R. Ruddle (Eds.), People and Computers XVIII-Design for Life: Proceedings of HCI 2004. London: Springer-Verlag Ltd.

Prensky, M. (2006). *Don't bother me mom—I'm learning*. St. Paul, MN: Paragon House.

Prensky, M. (2010). *Teaching digital natives—Partnering for real learning*. Thousand Oaks, CA: Corwin.

Ratey, J., & Hagerman, H. (2008). *Spark—The revolutionary new science of exercise and the brain*. New York: Little, Brown and Company.

Rayner, K. (1998). *Eye movements in reading and information processing: 20 years of research*. Psychological Bulletin, 124, 372-422.

Richardson, W. (2008). *Blogs, wikis, podcasts, and other powerful web tools for classrooms*. Thousand Oaks, CA: Corwin.

Rideout, V. & Hamel, E. (2006). *The media family: Electronic media in the lives of infants, toddlers, preschoolers, school age children and their parents*. Chestnut Hill, MA: Boston College.

Sexton, J. (2009). *Doesn't graphic design/layout affect scanning patterns?* http://www.grokdotcom.com/2009/04/08/doesnt-graphic-designlayout-affect-scanning-patterns/

Shirky, C. (2008). *Here comes everybody: The power of organizing with organizations*. New York: Penguin Press.

Singleton, D., & Lengyl, Z. (1995). *The Age Factor in Second Language Acquisition*. Bristol, UK: Multilingual Matters Ltd.

Small, G., & Vorgon, G. (2008). *iBrain: Surviving the technological alteration of the modern mind*. New York: Harper Collins.

Sousa, D. (2005). *How the brain learns*. Thousand Oaks, CA: Corwin.

Tapscott, D. (2008). *Wikinomics: How mass collaboration changes everything*. New York: McGraw-Hill.

Tapscott, D. (2009). *Grown up digital: How the net generation is changing your world*. New York: McGraw-Hill.

Trilling, B., & Fadel, C. (2009). *21st century skills: Learning for life in our times*. San Francisco: Jossey-Bass.

U.S. Census Bureau, (2007). *Current population survey, 2006: Annual social and economic supplement*. http://www.census.gov/apsd/techdoc/cps/cpsmar06.pdf

Wagner, T. (2008). *The global achievement gap: Why even our best schools don't teach the new survival skills our children need and what we can do about it*. New York: Basic Books.

Vangeliakos, C. (2007). *Neuroscience researchers expand usage of brainbow technology*. http://www.thecrimson.com/article/2007/11/2/neuroscience-researchers-expand-usage-of-brainbow/ Cambridge MA: Harvard Crimson.

Warlick, D. (2007). *F-Patterns and hot spots on web pages—* http://www.blackartofwebpublishing.com/FPatternHotSpots

Willingham, D. (2009). *Why don't students like school? A cognitive scientist answers questions about how the mind works and what it means for the classroom*. San Francisco: John Wiley and Sons.

Wurman, R. S. (2002). *Information anxiety*. New York: Hayden.

Zemke, R. (1985). *Computer literacy needs assessment—A trainer's guide*. New York: Addison Wesley.

Zittrain, J. (2008). *The future of the Internet—And how to stop it*. New York: Yale University Press.

Index

L

M

N

W

Y

Z